Worship Planning
Resources for
Every Sunday of the Year

# The Abingdon
# Worship Annual

# 2025

Edited by

## Mary Scifres
## and B. J. Beu

Abingdon Press / Nashville

THE ABINGDON WORSHIP ANNUAL 2025:
WORSHIP PLANNING RESOURCES
FOR EVERY SUNDAY OF THE YEAR

*Copyright © 2024 by Abingdon Press*

All rights reserved.

ISBN 978-1-7910-3226-5

All lectionary verses and all Scripture quotations, unless noted otherwise, are taken from the Common English Bible (CEB), copyright 2011. Used by permission. All rights reserved.

Scripture quotations marked NRSVUE are taken from the New Revised Standard Version Updated Edition. Copyright © 2021 National Council of Churches of Christ in the United States of America. Used by permission. All rights reserved worldwide.

MANUFACTURED IN THE UNITED STATES OF AMERICA

# Contents

# May

# June

# July

# August

# September

# October

# November

# December

# Introduction

The worship landscape has changed so much in recent years that many worship leaders are feeling overwhelmed. Pastors and worship leaders find themselves faced with expectations to match the quality and polish of mega churches that have vast resources and talent pool, whereas most mainline pastors serve churches of fewer than 200 members and a small pool of talent and resources to draw from. Planning and leading worship is a high calling as we seek to increase people's awareness of God's presence in their lives, create space for the Holy to move and breathe into our worship gatherings, and offer a quality experience of sacred worship.

With expectations high and resources often limited, we offer this resource as a way of simplifying your planning and supporting your ministry. *The Abingdon Worship Annual 2025* serves as a resource and partner in your planning process. In this resource, we provide theme ideas and all the written and spoken elements of worship, following the Revised Common Lectionary. Here, you will find words for worship to provide the framework for congregations to participate fully in the liturgical life of worship.

In *The Abingdon Worship Annual 2025*, you will find the words of many different authors, poets, pastors, laypersons, and theologians. Some authors have written for this resource before; others provide a fresh voice. Since the contributing authors represent a wide variety of denominational and theological backgrounds, their words will vary in style and content. Feel free to combine or adjust the words within these pages to fit the needs of your congregation and the style of your worship. (Notice the reprint and broadcast permission for worship given on the copyright page of this book.)

Each entry provides suggestions that follow an order of service that may be adapted to address your specific worship practice and format. Feel free to re-order or pick and choose the various resources to fit the needs of your worship services and congregations. Each entry follows a thematic focus arising from one or more of the week's scriptures.

To fit the Basic Pattern of Christian Worship—reflecting a flow that leads from a time of gathering and praise, into a time of receiving and responding to the Word, and ending with a time of sending forth—each entry includes Centering Words, Call to Worship and Opening Prayer, Prayer of Confession or Yearning and Words of Assurance, Response to the Word, Offering Prayer, and Benedictions. Communion Resources and other litanies and prayers are offered in selected entries.

Use the words offered here in the way the best suits your congregation's spiritual needs, on screen, in print, and in online worship; and please remember to give copyright and author credit!

## Using the Worship Resources

**Centering Words** focus the people on the day's theme. These can be used in email introductions to invite people to worship, on screen or in the bulletin as people arrive for worship, or spoken aloud to center people's thoughts and minds on the day's focus.

**Calls to Worship** gather God's people together as they prepare to worship. Often called "Greetings" or "Gathering Words," these words may be read by one worship leader or be read responsively. Regardless of how they are printed in this resource, feel free to experiment in your services of worship. They may be read antiphonally (back and forth) between two readers or two groups within the congregation: choir and musicians, young people and old, right side and left side, and so on.

**Opening Prayers** in this resource are varied in form but typically invoke God's presence into worship. Whether formal, informal, general, or specific, these prayers serve to attune our hearts and minds to God. Although many may be adapted for use in other parts of the worship service, we have grouped them into the category "Opening Prayers."

**Prayers of Confession** or **Prayers of Yearning** and **Words of Assurance** lead the people of God to acknowledge our yearning to be closer to God and closer to God's call in our lives while assuring us of God's forgiveness and grace. Regardless of how they are printed, whether unison or responsively, these prayers and words may be spoken by a single leader or led by a small group. Some prayers may even be used as Opening or Closing Prayers.

**Litanies** and **Responsive Readings** offer additional avenues of congregational participation in our services of worship. Think creatively as you decide how to use these **Responsive Readings** in your service of worship: in unison, by a worship leader alone, or in a call and response format. Feel free to change the title of these liturgies to sit your worship setting.

**Benedictions**, sometimes called "Blessings" or "Words of Dismissal," send the congregation forth to continue the work of worship. Some of these Benedictions work best in call and response format; others work best when delivered as a blessing by a single worship leader. As always, use the format best suited to your congregation.

In response to requests from many of our readers, we have provided a number of **Communion** liturgies as well, each written specifically to relate to the thematic and scriptural focus of the day. Some follow the pattern of the Great Thanksgiving; others are Invitations to Communion or Communion Prayers of Consecration for the celebration of the Eucharist. For a more extensive set of communion resources, see our free offer at https://maryscifres.simplero.com/communionbook.

## Adapting Liturgy for Online Worship

When worshiping on-line, some of our former traditions don't work as well in the virtual world. For responsive readings, inviting two leaders to read back and forth (rather than awaiting a congregation's unison response) can be much more effective when live streaming or video conferencing worship gatherings. Similarly, unison readings are less effective on-line due to buffering and delays that on-line brings to any attempt at unison reading or singing. Instead, we encourage single readers—preferably various laypeople throughout the church year—to lead "unison" moments while others are encouraged to read along quietly, silently, or aloud with one another in their homes while being muted online. If live streaming, intentionally add a moment of pause before and after any unison "in person" moments for the time delay that live streamers often experience as they worship from other locations. The moment of pause helps unify both congregations, while also allowing the gentle breath of the Holy Spirit to breathe a pause into our worshiping rhythm. Feel free to share the prayers and readings from within these pages, not only on-line but in weekly e-newsletters or devotionals. Note the copyright and authorship, and then share with your people in creative ways to nourish their spiritual journeys. Let us know if you have questions on how to innovate your use of liturgy and worship words. We really do want to support and strengthen your ministry and your congregation's worship life.

## Adapting Virtual Worship to a Hybrid Form

Over these last few years, you have likely led worship in a variety of ways, adapting to social restrictions the pandemic has thrown our way. We have begun calling this new *both-and* situation *hybrid worship.* Our worship services are no longer just the old fossil-fueled combustion engine of sanctuary worship, but also electric-fueled worship of videos streamed directly into the homes of church members and friends around the globe. One colleague welcomed a North Carolina family into membership in his California church 3000 miles away. When their sanctuary re-opened, the North Carolina family continued to participate and connect through the many online worship and study group opportunities of their California church home, growing more and more deeply connected regardless of geographical distance. As congregations again gather for in-person worship, this hybrid model allows us to continue serving our virtual worshipers. To prepare for this, worship leaders have put tech crews in place who can record the services, upload to an on-line platform, and communicate with the congregation how to access the on-line service. Your best practice is for worship leaders to focus on the worship components (music, message, liturgy) and for tech and administrative team members to focus on the technology and communication components. Let us know if you have questions or concerns we can help you address, or if you have insights and ideas to share with others.

## Companion Resources

Although you will find *The Abingdon Worship Annual 2025* an invaluable tool for planning worship, it is but one piece of the puzzle for worship preparation. For additional music suggestions, you will want to consult *Prepare! An Ecumenical Music and Worship Planner*, or *The United Methodist Music and Worship Planner*. These resources contain lengthy listings of lectionary-related hymns, praise songs, vocal solos, and choral anthems. For more communion resources, enjoy a free sample of B. J.'s and Mary's book *Is It Communion Sunday Already?!* by visiting https://maryscifres.simplero .com/communionbook.

As a final complement to your worship planning process, Mary also pens *Creative Worship Made Easy*, a resource of theme-based worship ideas including video and film clip suggestions, screen visuals, popular song ideas, hands-on participation suggestions, along with series ideas, suggested sermon titles, and sermon starters for each Sunday. Explore Mary's *Worship Resource Subscription* **Creative Worship Made Easy** at creativeworshipmadeeasy.com.

As you begin your worship planning, read the scriptures for each day, then meditate on the **Theme Ideas** suggested in this resource. Review the many words for worship printed herein and listen for the words that speak to you. Trust God's guidance, and enjoy a wonderful year of worship and praise!

Mary Scifres and B. J. Beu, Editors
*The Abingdon Worship Annual*
beuscifres@gmail.com

# January 1, 2025

## Watch Night / New Year's

### Kristiane Smith

## COLOR

White

## SCRIPTURE READINGS

Ecclesiastes 3:1-13; Psalm 8; Revelation 21:1-6a;
Matthew 25:31-46

## THEME IDEAS

Today's readings center on God's new beginnings. They
share an awareness of what can happen when God,
love, and justice culminate in the holy city coming from
heaven to earth. F. E. Weatherly's "The Holy City" cap-
tures this vision—a vision of a place where no one is
turned away: "I saw the Holy City beside the tideless
sea. The light of gold was on its streets, the gates were
open wide and all who would might enter, and no one
was denied." As you prepare for worship today, may
Weatherly's words tie our scripture readings in a nice,
pretty bow. As we begin this new year, let us dream together of a world where no one is denied.

# INVITATION AND GATHERING

### CENTERING WORDS (Matthew 25)

As the calendar changes, experience the restorative presence of God. As we renew our bodies, minds, and spirits, let us welcome the stranger and feed the hungry as if we were already family.

### CALL TO WORSHIP (Ecclesiastes 3, Matthew 25)

Today brings renewal to our lives.
**We will see with fresh eyes.**
Today brings fresh promises.
**We will be vulnerable to new ideas.**
Today brings new opportunities to share.
**We will welcome the stranger**
**through kinship with Christ.**

### OPENING PRAYER (Ecclesiastes 3, Revelation 21)

Maker of all things new, as we enter into worship,
we are excited for what comes next.
You have a time and purpose
for everyone we encounter
and for every season under heaven.
Help us see with new eyes and hear with new ears,
that we might leave with a new understanding
of what brings heaven to earth.
In Christ's name, we pray. Amen.

# PROCLAMATION AND RESPONSE

### PRAYER OF YEARNING (Revelation 21)

God of all peoples, we long to see you
in the lives of others,
but we sometimes fail to see past
our own limited views.

Open our eyes to see the needs around us,
as we feed the hungry, house the unhoused,
and are Christ's hands and feet
to a nation in need.
By living into your example,
may everyone we encounter
see Jesus within us. Amen

*WORDS OF ASSURANCE (Psalm 8)*
We see God's handiwork in the heavens
and it's celestial glory.
Greater still is God's love for us.

*PASSING THE PEACE OF CHRIST (Ecclesiastes 3)*
God has tasked us to bring the joy of Christ to all. Let us
greet one another in agape love.

*RESPONSE TO THE WORD (Matthew 25)*
What should we do, Lord?
Where do we begin?
You have told us to feed the hungry,
visit the imprisoned, welcome the stranger,
and provide food and drink
to those who hunger and thirst.
When this is done, your kingdom becomes real,
in our world and in our lives. Amen.

# THANKSGIVING AND COMMUNION

*OFFERING PRAYER (Matthew 25)*
We offer you these gifts
in gratitude for all you have done.
May our offering be used to help those in need,
so that our church may continue your work
in the world. Amen.

# SENDING FORTH

**BENEDICTION**
> Let us take the joy we have experienced today with us,
>> knowing that God's love is greater than our failings.
> Through God's teaching in Christ Jesus,
>> may we experience the new Jerusalem,
>> where everyone is welcome and has enough.

Notes

# January 5, 2025

## Epiphany of the Lord

### Mary Scifres
*Copyright © Mary Scifres*

## COLOR

White

## SCRIPTURE READINGS

Isaiah 60:1-6; Psalm 72:1-7, 10-14; Ephesians 3:1-12;
Matthew 2:1-12

## THEME IDEAS

Today's scriptures invite us to celebrate the gift of gift-giving. Isaiah and Matthew proclaim the honor of kings bringing gifts to the King, as does Psalm 72. But Psalm 72 takes it to a deeper level, praying that judgment and righteousness be given to the king, that the king may bring justice and righteousness to his people. And Paul celebrates the most precious gift King Jesus could ever offer—the gift of grace. What gifts might we bring to celebrate and honor the King?

# INVITATION AND GATHERING

**CENTERING WORDS** *(Ephesians 3, Matthew 2)*
What gift shall we bring to treasure honor King Jesus,
who honors us with the gifts of love and grace?

**CALL TO WORSHIP or INVITATION TO THE OFFER-
ING** *(Isaiah 60, Matthew 2)*
Bring your gifts and bring your love
to honor the King of love.
**Bring your worship and bring your praise
to pay homage to Christ Jesus, our King.**

**OPENING PRAYER** *(Matthew 2)*
Gracious God, we come into your presence
with joy and praise,
grateful for the gift of Christ Jesus in our lives.
As we celebrate this gift in our service of worship,
fill our hearts with Christmas joy
and our spirits with the gift of your Holy Spirit.
With joy and gratitude, we pray. Amen.

# PROCLAMATION AND RESPONSE

**PRAYER OF YEARNING** *(Ephesians 3, Matthew 2)*
Christ Jesus, we yearn for your grace to fill our lives.
We yearn to accept your love so fully
that our hearts might overflow with love
for your world.
Gift us, not just with your mercy and grace,
but with an openness and confidence
to receive your gifts.
Shine through our hearts, our lives, and our actions,
that others may find in us
generous friends of grace and love.

May our prayers and our actions
bring your light and love to the world. Amen.

*WORDS OF ASSURANCE (Ephesians 3, Matthew 2)*
In Christ's grace, we can boldly embrace God's love.
In Christ's mercy, we can confidently proclaim
that God's love is enough.

*PASSING THE PEACE OF CHRIST (Psalm 72)*
May peace prosper among us until the moon is no more.
May we share signs of peace and love to sustain us in
this New Year.

*INTRODUCTION TO THE WORD (Psalm 72)*
May God's word fall upon us,
refreshing us with hope for the new year.
May God's word fall upon us,
nourishing us with grace and love for God's world.
May God's word fall upon us,
challenging us to acts of justice and compassion.

*RESPONSE TO THE WORD (Psalm 72)*
Lift your eyes and see those in need of God's justice.
**We will lift our hearts to those who need
of Christ's compassion.**
Lift your hands and help those in need
of justice and compassion.
**We will gift the world with Christ's light,
in both word and action.**

# THANKSGIVING AND COMMUNION

*INVITATION TO THE OFFERING (Isaiah 60, Matthew 2)*
On this day of celebration, let us bring our gifts, as sages
of old once brought gifts to Christ the King. May our
gifts become the light of Christ for the world.

**OFFERING PRAYER** *(Isaiah 60, Matthew 2)*
Generous God, thank you for the gift of Jesus.
Thank you for the gifts of Christmas.
Thank you for inviting us to bring gifts to your world.
Bless the gifts we bring,
that they may become vessels
of Christ's light and love in the world. Amen.

**INVITATION TO COMMUNION** *(Isaiah 60, Ephesians 3)*
Arise; shine, for the light of Christ is shining
upon and within us.
**Arise; receive, for the grace of Christ is flowing
in and through these gifts.**
Gather around.
**These gifts are available to all.**

**PRAYER OF CONSECRATION** *(Ephesians 3, Isaiah 60)*
God of grace and glory,
pour out your power and presence
on these gifts of bread and wine.
May they be for us the very presence
of Christ in our midst.
Pour out your power and presence on us,
that we may become Christ for your world:
Light upon light,
Grace upon grace,
Gift upon gift,
for all the world to know and receive.
Amen.

# SENDING FORTH

**BENEDICTION** *(Isaiah 60, Ephesians 3)*
Arise; shine!
**The world needs our light.**

Go forth with grace and love.
**Every person needs our grace and love.**
Go forth with the gift of Christ's presence.
**Christ's presence will save us all. Amen.**

Notes

# January 12, 2025

## Baptism of the Lord

### Mary Petrina Boyd

## COLOR

White

## SCRIPTURE READINGS

Isaiah 43:1-7; Psalm 29; Acts 8:14-17; Luke 3:15-17, 21-22

## THEME IDEAS

Water and fire flow through these passages. Both elements have the power to destroy and the power to sustain life. In God's hands, water and fire are signs of the Holy Spirit. God's love keeps us safe and secure. As we hear the story of Jesus' baptism, we remember that we too are baptized and dwell safe in God's loving embrace.

## INVITATION AND GATHERING

**CENTERING WORDS** *(Isaiah 43, Psalm 29, Luke 3)*
The waters of God's blessing flow through our lives, quenching our thirst, bringing forth new hope.

*CALL TO WORSHIP (Isaiah 43, Psalm 29, Luke 3)*
We hear God's voice.
    **It thunders through creation.**
God's voice is strong.
    **It shatters the cedars of Lebanon.**
God is still speaking.
    **Calling out our names.**
Listen for God.
    **God calls us beloved.**

    ~or~

*CALL TO WORSHIP (Luke 3)*
Come to the waters.
    **We gather at the river.**
Come to the waters.
    **The waters of grace flow over us.**
Come to the waters.
    **We are washed in God's love.**
Come to the waters.
    **We are God's beloved children.**

*OPENING PRAYER (Isaiah 43, Luke 3)*
God of strength, God of love,
    surround us with your love.
Gather us in as your beloved children.
Open our ears to hear your voice.
Open our hearts to the power of your transforming love.
May your waters of grace pour over us,
    renewing us for your work in the world.
Bless us in this holy time. Amen.

# PROCLAMATION AND RESPONSE

**PRAYER OF YEARNING (Isaiah 43)**
> Loving God, sometimes life seems overwhelming.
> There is so much happening that we can't control.
> We feel like we are drowning.
> Then we hear your voice saying, "Don't fear,"
> > and we remember that your love supports
> > > and sustains us.
> You are there when we feel overwhelmed.
> You are there when we struggle.
> You give us what we need.
> Help us place our trust in you,
> > as we step away from fear,
> > > secure in your love. Amen.

**WORDS OF ASSURANCE (Isaiah 43)**
> God says, "Don't be afraid."
> God calls and names us as God's own.

**PASSING THE PEACE OF CHRIST (Psalm 29)**
> Peace is a gift of God's love. Let the Lord bless us and
> give us strength, as we share signs of this peace!

**INTRODUCTION TO THE WORD (Luke 3)**
> At the banks of the Jordan River, everyone was filled
> with expectation. John told them that one was coming
> who had greater power than his own. May we too be
> filled with expectation, as we hear God's word today.

**RESPONSE TO THE WORD (Isaiah 43, Luke 3—based on
UMC baptismal vows.)**
> In the silence, God, we listen for your voice.
> We hear you say, "Don't be afraid,"
> > and we dare to resist evil, injustice, and oppression.

We hear you say, "You are my child,"
    and we find courage to serve
        as Christ's representatives in the world.
We hear you say, "You are my beloved,"
    and we live in joy, sharing your peace.
We hear you and we thank you for your gift of love.
Amen.

# THANKSGIVING AND COMMUNION

### INVITATION TO THE OFFERING (Isaiah 43, Luke 3)
We live in security, trusting God's abundant care. Let us
give with joy, serving Jesus Christ, God's beloved child.

### OFFERING PRAYER (Isaiah 43)
Loving God, you bless us with your love.
You know each one of us.
We live in confidence and trust,
    knowing your care for us.
We bring these gifts to you, our source of life.
Use them, we pray,
    that others may experience your grace
        and live free from fear. Amen.

### INVITATION TO COMMUNION (Luke 3)
Come to the table of love.
    **Jesus meets us here.**
We gather as the beloved community,
    **hungry to be fed with the gifts of the spirit,**
    **thirsting for the waters of life.**
God is here and everyone is welcome.

# SENDING FORTH

**BENEDICTION *(Isaiah 43, Psalm 29, Luke 3)***
God knows your names.
As God's beloved children,
    you belong to God.
Secure in this love, go forth to live without fear,
    trusting God's abundant care,
    resting in God's peace.

# ADDITIONAL RESOURCES

**LITANY *(Isaiah 43)***
*(Sing a verse of "How Firm a Foundation" between responses.)*
Our God, who created us and formed us, speaks:
    *"How firm a foundation, ye saints of the Lord,*
    *is laid for your faith in his excellent word!*
    *What more can he say than to you he hath said,*
    *to you who for refuge to Jesus have fled?"*
Don't fear, for I have redeemed you.
I have called you by name; you are mine.
    *"Fear not, I am with thee, O be not dismayed,*
    *for I am thy God and will still give thee aid;*
    *I'll strengthen and help thee,*
        *and cause thee to stand*
    *upheld by my righteous, omnipotent hand."*
When you pass through the waters, I will be with you.
The rivers won't sweep over you.
    *"When through the deep waters I call thee to go,*
    *the rivers of woe shall not thee overflow;*
    *for I will be with thee, thy troubles to bless,*
    *and sanctify to thee thy deepest distress."*

When you walk through the fire, you won't be scorched
and flame won't burn you.

*"When through fiery trials*
   *thy pathways shall lie,*
*my grace, all-sufficient, shall be thy supply;*
*the flame shall not hurt thee; I only design*
*thy dross to consume, and thy gold to refine."*

You are precious in my eyes, you are honored,
and I love you.

*"The soul that on Jesus still leans for repose,*
*I will not, I will not desert to its foes;*
*that soul, though all hell*
   *should endeavor to shake,*
*I'll never, no, never, no, never forsake."*

Don't fear; I am with you.

Notes

# January 19, 2025

## Second Sunday after the Epiphany

### Mary Scifres
*Copyright © Mary Scifres*

## COLOR

Green

## SCRIPTURE READINGS

Isaiah 62:1-5; Psalm 36:5-10; 1 Corinthians 12:1-11;
John 2:1-11

## THEME IDEAS

God's steadfast love manifests in a variety of ways, but
steadfast and true it always is. Whether reclaiming us
when we have wandered (Isaiah 62), imparting gifts
through the power of God's Holy Spirit (1 Corinthians 12), or transforming water into wine at a wedding
celebration (John 2), God's love flows abundantly. The
steadiness of God's love can be the assurance we need
to return after we have wandered, to claim and utilize
the gifts we are given, and to rejoice in a celebration,
even when supplies run short.

# INVITATION AND GATHERING

**CENTERING WORDS *(Psalm 36)***
God's steadfast love endures forever.

**CALL TO WORSHIP *(Psalm 36, 1 Corinthians 12)***
God's faithful love welcomes us here.
**Thank God for this glorious gift!**
God's faithful love redeems our lives.
**Thank God for our many blessings!**
God's faithful love is ours to share.
**We will offer this gift to God's world.**

**OPENING PRAYER *(Isaiah 62, Psalm 36, 1 Corinthians 12)***
Faithful God, we come to you from many walks of life.
Some of us come after wandering off.
Others come sensing that you are as close
    as their very breath.
From our many journeys,
    welcome us with your love.
Pour out your Holy Spirit on us,
    that we might sense your presence in our lives.
In joyous gratitude, we pray. Amen.

# PROCLAMATION AND RESPONSE

**PRAYER OF YEARNING *(Isaiah 62, Psalm 36,***
***1 Corinthians 12)***
Beloved One, thank you for loving us.
Help us sense your steadfast love,
    even when we feel unsure or unworthy.
Help us sense your presence,
    especially when we are feel alone.
Guide us home when we wander off.

Claim us as your delight and your crown of beauty,
    that we might shine with your love
        and readily share your gifts with others. Amen.

**WORDS OF ASSURANCE (*Isaiah 62, Psalm 36,
1 Corinthians 12*)**
    You are no longer abandoned, deserted, or defeated.
    In God's steadfast love,
        and through the Spirit's powerful presence,
        you are claimed as God's delight.
    You are gifted to serve God's world with love.

**INTRODUCTION TO THE WORD (*Isaiah 62, Psalm 36,
John 2*)**
    Listen for God's miraculous message of love.

**RESPONSE TO THE WORD (*Isaiah 62, 1 Corinthians 12*)**
    Gifted in unique and beautiful ways,
      **we are blessed by God's Holy Spirit.**
    Gifted to serve and share,
      **we are blessed by God's trust.**
    Gifted to be God's delight and crown of beauty,
      **we are blessed to be Christ for the world.**
    We are the body of Christ.
      **Let us rejoice and live into this truth.**

# THANKSGIVING AND COMMUNION

**INVITATION TO THE OFFERING (*1 Corinthians 12*)**
    As we offer our material gifts in this time of offering,
let's also reflect and rejoice in the time, talents, and spiritual gifts with which we are blessed. Let us share abundantly from every aspect of our lives.

**OFFERING PRAYER** *(Psalm 36, 1 Corinthians 12)*
God of steadfast love and faithfulness,
thank you for the gift of your love
and the gifts of your Holy Spirit.
Thank you for the gifts we return to you,
this day and every day.
Help us share as generously with others
as you have shared with us,
that your love might be known
throughout all the world. Amen.

# SENDING FORTH

**BENEDICTION** *(Isaiah 62, 1 Corinthians 12, John 2)*
As miracles of God, go to be God's miracle for the world.
**We are blessed with God's gifts.**
Let's share those gifts with the world.
**Amen and amen.**

*(For ideas related to John 2, consult* **The Abingdon Worship Annual 2022** *or visit creativeworshipmadeeasy.com.)*

# Notes

# January 26, 2025

## Third Sunday after the Epiphany

### B. J. Beu
Copyright © B. J. Beu

## COLOR

Green

## SCRIPTURE READINGS

Nehemiah 8:1-3, 5-6, 8-10; Psalm 19;
1 Corinthians 12:12-31a; Luke 4:14-21

## THEME IDEAS

According to the psalmist, day and night pour forth
speech and reveal knowledge, but no words can contain their truth (Psalm 19:2). Additionally, God's law is
perfect, reviving the soul. The very decrees of the Lord
make the wise simple (v.7). How do we understand
these teachings? When shared by creation, do we even
know how to listen? When Nehemiah read the Book
of the Law of Moses to the people, he had to give the
meaning so that they would understand. In Corinth,
Paul looked for the Spirit to bind the church together
through the power of Christian baptism, because teachings on Christian unity were falling on deaf ears. Even
the people in Jesus' hometown could not see the truth

of who he was, as Jesus read from the scroll of Isaiah. The very heavens reveal the knowledge of our God, and the precepts of God in scripture are perfect, but without help understanding them, we often remain blissfully unaware.

# INVITATION AND GATHERING

**CENTERING WORDS** *(Nehemiah 8, Psalm 19)*
The joy of the Lord is our strength. The Word of God is our joy.

**CALL TO WORSHIP** *(Nehemiah 8, Psalm 19)*
Day pours forth speech and night declares knowledge.
**What voices speak without words or speech?**
The heavens are telling the glory of God.
**We listen but do not understand.**
The Law of God is perfect, reviving the soul.
**Who will teach us, that our hearts may rejoice?**
Pray in the Spirit and you will perceive.

**OPENING PRAYER** *(Nehemiah 8, Psalm 19, Luke 4)*
God of Wisdom, we have come to sit at Jesus' feet
and learn to what he would teach us.
With the heavens above and the earth below,
we rejoice in the good news he brings:
succor to the poor, release to the captives,
recovery of sight to the blind,
and freedom for the oppressed.
Reveal the mystery of your precepts,
that we might hear the music of the heavens—
the whisper of the land and roar of the seas,
the prayer of the caterpillar and song of the flea.
Speak to us through the fullness of creation, we pray.
Amen.

23

# PROCLAMATION AND RESPONSE

**PRAYER OF YEARNING** *(Nehemiah, Psalm 19,*
*1 Corinthians 12, Luke 14)*
>Merciful God, as we seek to know your ways,
>>may we be more ready to receive the gifts of others
>>>than to trumpet the gifts we have received.
>Lay your call to Christian unity on our hearts,
>>as we listen to your precepts
>>>and seek to live them each day.
>As the heavens proclaim your praise,
>>and the day and the night reveal your truth,
>>>open our hearts to those who need our care.
>Amen.

**WORDS OF ASSURANCE** *(Nehemiah 8:10)*
>Hear the words of Nehemiah:
>>"Go your way, eat the fat and drink sweet wine
>>and send portions of them to those
>>for whom nothing is prepared,
>>for this day is holy to our LORD,
>>and do not be grieved,
>>for the joy of the LORD is your strength."

**PASSING THE PEACE OF CHRIST** *(Psalm 19)*
>The heavens above and every part of creation below reveals God's glory without speech. Look at one another in wonder and silently share the peace of Christ with a smile, bow, handshake, hug, or simple reverence.

**INTRODUCTION TO THE WORD** *(Psalm 19:14 NRSVUE)*
>"Let the words of my mouth and the meditation of my heart be acceptable to you, O Lord, my rock and my redeemer."

*RESPONSE TO THE WORD (Psalm 19)*
Listen! The heavens speak without words.
    **Give glory to our God!**
The sun and moon reveal lessons beyond price.
    **Sing praises to Christ Jesus!**
The wind whispers mysteries deeper than the sea.
    **Rejoice in the life-giving Spirit!**
Listen! And share what you hear.

# THANKSGIVING AND COMMUNION

*OFFERING PRAYER (Luke 4)*
God of our ancestors, Caretaker of our future,
    thank you for your faithful love.
May the gifts we bring before you this day
    honor the many ways you bless this church.
And may our offering reflect our commitment
    to lead lives of love, as we continue Jesus' mission
    to bring good new to the poor,
        release to the captives, sight to the blind,
        and freedom to the oppressed.
In your holy name, we pray. Amen.

# SENDING FORTH

*BENEDICTION (Psalm 19, 1 Corinthians 12)*
In one Spirit, we perceive the glory of God
proclaimed in the heavens above.
    **Spirit, make us one.**
In one faith, we have been nurtured
through the precepts of the living Lord.
    **Christ, make us one.**
In one great love, we have been saved.
    **God, make us one.**
Go with the blessing of God,
that all might be one.

# Notes

# February 2, 2025

## Fourth Sunday after the Epiphany

Mary Scifres
*Copyright © Mary Scifres*

## COLOR

Green

## SCRIPTURE READINGS

Jeremiah 1:4-10; Psalm 71:1-6; 1 Corinthians 13:1-13; Luke 4:21-30

## THEME IDEAS

Although these scriptures can all be viewed independently, some common themes emerge: the contrast of childlike and mature faith, the ageless values of answering God's call, trusting God's steadfast faithfulness, and focusing on love to guide us through all ages and seasons of life.

## INVITATION AND GATHERING

**CENTERING WORDS (1 Corinthians 13)**
Love guides the way through every season, in every situation, and in every life.

**CALL TO WORSHIP** *(Jeremiah 1, 1 Corinthians 13, Luke 4)*
Let us gather to listen deeply.
**Word of God, speak.**
Let us gather with childlike faith.
**Ageless wisdom, reveal.**
Word of God, speak.
**Your servants are listening.**

**OPENING PRAYER** *(Jeremiah 1, 1 Corinthians 13, Luke 4)*
God of love and life, speak to our hearts this day.
Speak words of wisdom and faith.
Open our hearts and minds
to perceive your message of love,
even when it's hard to hear.
Strengthen our faith to answer your call,
even when we don't feel confident or capable.
Be our wisdom, our strength, and our love,
that we may bring your wisdom, strength, and love
to the world. Amen.

# PROCLAMATION AND RESPONSE

**PRAYER OF YEARNING** *(1 Corinthians 13)*
Gracious, loving God,
pour your love into our hearts and lives.
Bless us with such overflowing grace
that your love might flow within us
and through us.
Be patient with our impatience.
Calm us with your patient love in all of our encounters.
Forgive us and fill us with your grace,
that we might extend loving forgiveness to others.
In your loving name, we pray. Amen.

*WORDS OF ASSURANCE (1 Corinthians 13)*
    Faith, hope, and love remain.
    But it is through the greatest of these, love,
        that we forgive and are forgiven.
    Thanks be to God.

*PASSING THE PEACE OF CHRIST (1 Corinthians 13)*
    Let us speak with words of love and with gestures of
    peace, as we share the peace of Christ with one another.

*RESPONSE TO THE WORD (Jeremiah 1,*
*1 Corinthians 13, Luke 4)*
    May our lives reflect the challenging messages
        of scripture.
    May love guide our path
        and may courage light our way.
    Amen.

# THANKSGIVING AND COMMUNION

*INVITATION TO THE OFFERING (1 Corinthians 13)*
    As a sign of our love for God, God's church, and God's
    creation, let us share our gifts and offerings.

*OFFERING PRAYER (1 Corinthians 13, Luke 4)*
    Bless these gifts, O God,
        with your love, your strength, and your presence.
    May the ministries this offering supports be a sign
        of your love, strength, and presence in the world.
    Amen.

*INVITATION TO COMMUNION*
    Come freely, for this table of grace is here for all.
    Come confidently, for this table of love offers blessings
        beyond our wildest dreams.

Come humbly, for this table is set by Christ,
who humbled himself to both live and die
in his great love for us.

### GREAT THANKSGIVING

Lift up your hearts!
**We lift them up to God!**
Celebrate God's love!
**It is right to give God our thanks and praise!**

We give thanks and praise to you,
God of love and grace!
We celebrate the creative presence
that called forth this glorious earth
and the heavens above.
We praise and glorify you
for creating us in your very image.
We celebrate the long history
you traveled with us, as you called us
to be your light and love for the world,
and as you claimed us as your own.
We are humbled and grateful for the many times
you guided us along the way—
reclaiming us in our grumbling,
redirecting us in our wandering,
comforting us in our loneliness,
and steadfastly loving us with your grace.
From ancient days and ancient voices,
you have shown us the path
of love, justice and righteousness.

And so, with your people on earth,
and all the company of heaven,
we praise your name
and join their unending hymn, saying:

**Holy, holy, holy Lord, God of power and might,
heaven and earth are full of your glory.
Hosanna in the highest. Blessed is the one
who comes in the name of the Lord.
Hosanna in the highest.**

In the fullness of time, you came to us
in the presence of Jesus, the Christ,
showing us the way of strength and trust,
calling us to discipleship,
and inviting us to walk the path of love.
Even when faced with impending death,
Christ gave thanks and blessed the fruit
of your good earth,
offering not only bread and wine,
but the bread of life and the wine of salvation.

We remember his prophetic words:
"Take, eat, this is my body, broken for you.
Take, drink. This is my life poured out for you
and for many."

As we walk this journey of life,
we remember these gifts,
as we proclaim the mystery of faith:
**Christ has died.
Christ is risen.
Christ will come again.**

## COMMUNION PRAYER
Pour out your Holy Spirit on us,
that we might be disciples of your love and grace.
Pour out your Holy Spirit
on these gifts of bread and wine,
that your life and love might flow through us.

Guide us in love by your Spirit,
    that we might be one with Christ,
        one with each other,
            and one in ministry to all the world,
                until Christ comes in final victory
                    and we feast at the heavenly banquet.
Through Jesus Christ,
    with the Holy Spirit in your holy Church,
        all honor and glory is yours, Almighty God,
            now and forever more.
    **Amen.**

## *GIVING THE BREAD AND CUP*
*(The bread and wine are given to the people with these or other words of blessing.)*
The life of Christ, revealed in you.
The love of Christ, flowing through you.

# SENDING FORTH

## *BENEDICTION (1 Corinthians 13, Luke 4)*
Go with the courage of Christ.
Go with the Spirit of love.
Go to answer God's call,
    wherever and however God leads.

**Notes**

# February 9, 2025

## Fifth Sunday after the Epiphany

### B. J. Beu
*Copyright © B. J. Beu*

## COLOR

Green

## SCRIPTURE READINGS

Isaiah 6:1-8, (9-13); Psalm 138; 1 Corinthians 15:1-11; Luke 5:1-11

## THEME IDEAS

Isaiah's face-to-face encounter with the Lord evokes the same response as Peter's encounter with Jesus on the water: they both feel unworthy to be in God's awesome and holy presence. Yet, despite these feelings of inadequacy, when faced with God's call, we are ultimately charged to respond with Isaiah: "Here I am; send me!" (v.8b). Today's readings include contrasting proclamations from God. Messages of woe and destruction in Isaiah are joined with messages of hope and salvation in Psalm 138, 1 Corinthians 15, and Luke 5. Whatever our circumstances may be, our proper response is to worship the One who brings life out of death and hope out of despair.

# INVITATION AND GATHERING

**CENTERING WORDS** *(Isaiah 6, Luke 5)*
> The voice of God calls us this day. Christ beckons us to
> leave our old lives behind. Will we heed? Will we follow?

**CALL TO WORSHIP** *(Psalm 138)*
> Give thanks to the Lord.
> **Sing God's praises.**
> Call on the Lord.
> **Seek God with hearts full of song.**

~or~

**CALL TO WORSHIP** *(Isaiah 6)*
> The voice of God is calling:
> "Whom shall I send?"
> **We are here to answer God's call.**
> The voice of Christ is calling:
> "Who will be my faithful disciples?"
> **We are here to answer Christ's call.**
> The voice of Spirit is calling:
> "Who will be a light to the nations?"
> **We are here. Send us, we pray!**

**OPENING PRAYER** *(Luke 5, Isaiah 6)*
> Your wisdom, Holy Mystery,
>> is as unfathomable as the deep,
>>> as alluring as the night sky.
> When all seems lost,
>> call us from the wreckage of our lives.
> Grant us the ability and the will to hear your call
>> and bless us with the grace
>>> to embrace your promised salvation.
> Help us face our fears,
>> that we might remain sure-footed
>>> on our journey of faith. Amen.

# PROCLAMATION AND RESPONSE

**PRAYER OF YEARNING (Isaiah 6, Luke 5)**
Almighty God, we are a people of unclean lips
and live among a people of unclean lips.
We are more accustomed to spreading gossip
than we are to singing, "Holy, holy, holy."
Yet, we long to me made new and whole this day.
Breathe your Holy Spirit upon us
and call us to follow you once more.
As the disciples left their fishing boats,
may we leave the comfort of familiar shores.
Work through us in the power of your Son,
that all people might be brought to your glory.
Amen.

**WORDS OF ASSURANCE (Isaiah 6, Luke 5)**
Hear the good news, our names have been written
in the book of life.
Thanks be to God!

**PASSING THE PEACE OF CHRIST (Isaiah 6, Luke 5)**
The Holy One invites us into relationships so deep that
they have the power to change our very being. Let us
turn to one another with this hope, as we share signs of
Christ's peace with one another.

**RESPONSE TO THE WORD (1 Corinthians 15, Luke 5)**
Loved as God's children . . .
**we walk in the footsteps of the saints.**
Called as Christ's disciples . . .
**we follow the Lord of life.**
Blessed by the Holy Spirit . . .
**we abide in God's presence.**

~or~

## RESPONSE TO THE WORD (Isaiah 6, Luke 5)

God has work for us to do.
**We don't feel worthy.**
God has plans for us.
**We don't feel ready.**
Through God, all things are possible.
**We will put our trust in God.**

# THANKSGIVING AND COMMUNION

## OFFERING PRAYER (Psalm 138)

With hearts full of love,
may our spirits sing your praise.
As we bring our offering before you this day,
bless us and our gifts,
that we may bring your holy presence
where it is needed most in your world.
In your holy name, we pray. Amen.

# SENDING FORTH

## BENEDICTION (Psalm 138, 1 Corinthians 15)

God is our strength. Receive it.
Christ is our hope. Embrace it.
The Spirit is our joy. Share it.

~or~

## BENEDICTION (Luke 5)

Do not fear the turbulent waters of faith.
**Christ is with us in the boat.**
Do not avoid the dangers of the deep.
**God is with us on the journey.**
Do not doubt your ability to reach the lost.
**The Spirit blesses us with a bountiful catch.**

# Notes

# February 16, 2025

## Sixth Sunday after the Epiphany
### Kirsten Linford

## COLOR
Green

## SCRIPTURE READINGS
Jeremiah 17:5-10; Psalm 1; I Corinthians 15:12-20; Luke 6:17-26

## THEME IDEAS
Jeremiah, the psalmist, and Luke contrast the decision to follow God's teachings/laws/ways with the choice to turn from them. We expect the message that blessing comes from pursuing God's wisdom, with suffering following when we depart from that wisdom. But Luke's text might make us wonder if we are *required* to suffer to be righteous. Must we martyr ourselves to be good, to be true, to be faithful? Or is Luke's text an invitation to seek a deeper meaning—to walk closely with God; to seek God's guidance; to depend on Christ's presence; to yearn for what matters most, that which satisfies and endures? What does it mean to be truly faithful in good times and hard ones? How are we meant to live? And what does this look like in daily life during the season of Epiphany?

39

# INVITATION AND GATHERING

**CENTERING WORDS** *(Jeremiah 17)*
>Blessed are those who trust the Lord, whose trust is in the Lord. They shall be like trees planted by water, sending out their roots by the stream. They shall not cease to bear fruit.

**CALL TO WORSHIP** *(Jeremiah 17, Psalm 1)*
>Happy are those who delight in God's ways,
>>**who set their hearts and minds**
>>**on the laws of God's love.**
>
>In the presence of the Holy, they are like trees
>planted by the waters of life.
>>**They are fed by enduring streams,**
>>**with roots that reach into the depths**
>>**of the soul.**
>
>They are nourished in times of drought
>and bring forth fruit in seasons of famine.
>>**Life shall spring forth as they walk each day**
>>**in the Way of peace.**

**OPENING PRAYER** *(Jeremiah 17, Psalm 1)*
>Holy One, when the road is dusty under our feet
>>and we find ourselves engulfed,
>>>you share with us the water of life.
>
>You plant our spirits
>>by the streams of your Being.
>
>You nourish our bodies
>>and replenish our souls.
>
>You challenge our minds
>>and guide our hearts.
>
>Lead us, again, O God,
>>into your presence with your prayers.
>
>Be with us, as your renewing love overflows
>>from our lives and our souls
>>>into the world. Amen.

# PROCLAMATION AND RESPONSE

## PRAYER OF YEARNING (Jeremiah 17, Psalm 1)

God of Mercy, whose presence is ever-living,
make us whole.
Lay your path before us,
for we are easily confused, distracted,
blown off course, and lost.
In the arid places of our lives—
the seasons when our hearts starve
and our souls are parched and dry—
lead us to your living waters
and the nourishment
of your ever-flowing streams.
Plant us and center us in the core of your mercy,
that we might soak up your grace
and touch the fullness of your Life,
this day and all days. Amen.

## WORDS OF ASSURANCE (Luke 6)

In every impoverished place,
every season of greatest longing,
God is with us.
In every instance of confusion or conundrum
when we cannot find our way,
God comes to be our guide.
For every moment when our hearts hunger,
when our souls thirst
and our minds and bodies cry out,
God plants us by streams of grace.
God overcomes our pain,
until there is only life,
only love, only joy. Amen.

41

### PASSING THE PEACE OF CHRIST (*Luke 6:20-21*)

Even in our greatest struggles, Christ says, "Blessed are you, for yours is the kin-dom of God. For all who hunger will be filled. And all who weep will rejoice and laugh."

### PRAYER OF PREPARATION (*Psalm 19*)

May the words of my mouth . . .
**and the meditations of our hearts**
**be acceptable in your sight, O Lord,**
**our strength and our redeemer. Amen.**

### RESPONSE TO THE WORD (*Psalm 1*)

Happy are we who study your word, O God,
who walk on your very path.
In your Word, we have heard life.
In your teaching, we have been led to delight.
May your Word be planted in our hearts.
May our souls be planted like trees
by the streams of your Spirit,
that our lives may bear the fruit
of your work and your worth. Amen.

# THANKSGIVING AND COMMUNION

### INVITATION TO THE OFFERING (*Luke 6*)

God has satisfied the hunger of both our bodies and our souls. Let us share our gifts with all God's creation, that weeping may turn to laughter, and struggle may turn to joy.

### OFFERING PRAYER (*Jeremiah 17, Psalm 1, Luke 6*)

Merciful God, you bless us beyond measure or belief.
May the gifts you have poured into our lives
overflow, spilling over into the world.
May these gifts nourish all who have need. Amen.

# SENDING FORTH

**BENEDICTION** *(Jeremiah 17, Psalm 1, Luke 6)*
People of God, blessed are you.
Go into the world, following the living God—
this day and all days. Amen.

Notes

# February 23, 2025

## Seventh Sunday after the Epiphany

### Sara Lambert

## COLOR

Green

## SCRIPTURE READINGS

Genesis 45:3-11, 15; Psalm 37:1-11, 39-40;
1 Corinthians 15:35-38, 42-50; Luke 6:27-38

## THEME IDEAS

The meeting of Joseph with his brothers is a story of choosing reconciliation over revenge. Joseph had all the power when they reunite, yet he shows mercy, protecting his people from likely death. Psalm 37 continues the theme of mercy, by reminding us that when we trust God, prosperity and justice follow. First Corinthians lies alongside this theme, showing the importance of comparing the perishable and imperishable. Flesh and blood die, forgiveness and mercy last. The Gospel gives us a recipe for a merciful and blessed life. When we give, we will also receive. We are to take the Golden Rule to the next step. Beyond the transactional level, Jesus asks that we should forgive first, love first, and give first. Do good and trust the Lord.

# INVITATION AND GATHERING

**CENTERING WORDS** *(Psalm 37, Luke 6, Genesis 45)*
Come into this place with a quiet heart. Be still before
God and wait patiently, for the Lord is merciful.

**CALL TO WORSHIP** *(Psalm 37, Genesis 45, Luke 6)*
In these uncertain times, we come together,
searching for peace.
> **We will be still before the Lord**
> **and wait patiently.**
We will open our hearts and minds,
that the Lord may show us mercy.
> **When we trust the Lord, we can do good things**
> **and live with one another in peace and security.**
The Lord is our refuge in times of trouble.
In God, we find forgiveness, mercy, and love.
> **We will be still before the Lord**
> **and wait patiently.**

~or~

**CALL TO WORSHIP** *(Psalm 37, Genesis 45, Luke 6)*
Take delight in the Lord and receive
the desires of your heart.
> **We will bring a generosity of spirit**
> **and sing the harmony of mercy.**
The meek shall inherit the land
and rejoice in God's love.
> **We praise the Lord of mercy,**
> **pouring it out for all.**
Do good and trust the Lord.
Love first; forgive first; give first.
> **We come to worship, to heed the Word,**
> **and to grow in faith and love.**

*OPENING PRAYER (Genesis 45, Luke 6, Psalm 37)*
Holy One, we come together to pause, pray, and praise.
Be with us in this place,
that we may touch your mercy.
You provide for us;
help us claim the power of your love
for our lives.
Help us to measure out grace,
shaking it together with forgiveness
and give them to others
as you would have us do. Amen.

# PROCLAMATION AND RESPONSE

*PRAYER OF YEARNING (Psalm 37, Genesis 45, Luke 6)*
Lord God, we come to you as imperfect creatures.
Like Joseph's brothers, we're afraid of the past
and are wary of the future.
Yet, we yearn to feel your warm embrace.
We long to touch your love and forgiveness,
despite our shortcomings.
Ease our journey toward mercy,
as we grow in faith and love.
Help us bless those who curse us
and to pray for those who mistreat us.
This is your direction for our lives
and we will follow as we are able. Amen.

*WORDS OF ASSURANCE (Psalm 37, Luke 6)*
God's love and mercy are freely available to all.
When we trust and delight in God's mercy,
we are better able to show this mercy
to those around us.
Because God can do this, you can do it.
We can do it together!

*PASSING THE PEACE OF CHRIST (Genesis 45, Psalm 37, Luke 6)*

> May the peace of Christ find you on your journey toward grace and mercy. May the grace of forgiveness and the kindness of mercy dwell in your hearts today.

*RESPONSE TO THE WORD (Luke 6)*

> Measure a good amount of grace,
>> press it down and add more.
>
> Shake it together until it runs over with forgiveness.
> Then cook up a recipe for a merciful
>> and faithful life.

~or~

*RESPONSE TO THE WORD (Psalm 37)*

> Trust the Lord and delight in God's mercy.
> Bless those who curse you
>> and pray for those who mistreat you.
>
> Make mercy a part of who you are
>> in your journey toward peace.

# THANKSGIVING AND COMMUNION

*OFFERING PRAYER (Genesis 45, Luke 6, Psalm 37)*

> Holy God, we bring this offering
>> of our money, prayer, and labor
>>> to advance your work of mercy.
>
> We willingly and joyfully celebrate your generosity,
>> by sharing our abundance with the church,
>>> our community, and the world.
>
> Bless these gifts,
>> as they go forth to do good in your world
>>> without judgment or prejudice. Amen.

# SENDING FORTH

**BENEDICTION (*Genesis 45, Psalm 37, Luke 6*)**
May the peace of Christ follow you from this place.
Remember the grace of Joseph, the mercy of God,
and the love of Christ.
Go beyond the Golden Rule and forgive first, love first,
and give first.
Measure out a good amount of grace,
for you and others,
and prepare a recipe for a merciful life.

Notes

# March 2, 2025

## Transfiguration Sunday

### Mary Scifres
*Copyright © Mary Scifres*

## COLOR

White

## SCRIPTURE READINGS

Exodus 34:29-35; Psalm 99; 2 Corinthians 3:12–4:2;
Luke 9:28-36, (37-43a)

## THEME IDEAS

The revelation of God's glory intermingles with the glorification of God's followers in today's readings. Not only is Jesus transfigured before the disciples' eyes, they are brought into a new level of understanding of Jesus' greatness and glory. Just as Moses reveals God's instructions by bringing the tablets of the covenant to the Hebrew people, Jesus' transfiguration reveals a new understanding of who Jesus is to his disciples. The letter to the Corinthians pulls these ideas together, reminding us that God's glory has not only been revealed to us in Christ, but is being revealed through us as disciples of Christ.

49

# INVITATION AND GATHERING

**CENTERING WORDS** *(2 Corinthians 3, Luke 9, Transfiguration)*
> As God's glory shone in and through Christ Jesus, may God's glory shine in and through us with the beauty and grace of Christ's love.

**CALL TO WORSHIP** *(Luke 9, 2 Corinthians 3, Transfiguration)*
> Christ has called us here,
> > **inviting us to offer praise and prayer.**
> May Christ's presence be revealed in this time,
> > **showing us the way to go.**
> May Christ's glory shine into our worship,
> > **that Christ's glory may shine in our lives.**

**OPENING PRAYER** *(Luke 9, 2 Corinthians 3, Transfiguration)*
> God of glory and power,
> > pour out your Holy Spirit on us today.
> Reveal to us your wisdom and guidance.
> Manifest through us your Spirit of glorious grace
> > and love.
> And make your loving presence known to all,
> > through the ministries of your church. Amen.

# PROCLAMATION AND RESPONSE

**PRAYER OF YEARNING** *(Luke 9, 2 Corinthians 3, Transfiguration)*
> Gracious God, we tremble in the presence
> > of your glory and power.
> Strengthen our courage,

that we might look upon your love
and stop shrinking away in fear.
Embolden us to trust your grace,
no matter how grave our transgressions
or ashamed our hearts may be.
Shine upon us with your mercy,
that we may shine for all to see.
Grant us confidence in both your grace
and your abundant love.
In your loving name, we pray. Amen.

**WORDS OF ASSURANCE (2 Corinthians 3, 2 Corinthians 4)**
By God's mercy, we are redeemed and renewed
to shine with the love of Christ.
Thanks be to God.

**RESPONSE TO THE WORD or BENEDICTION (Luke 9, 2 Corinthians 3)**
With Christ's love,
**let us shine.**
With God's glory,
**let us shine.**
With the Spirit's power,
**let us shine.**

# THANKSGIVING AND COMMUNION

**OFFERING PRAYER (Luke 9, 2 Corinthians 3, Transfiguration)**
Glorious God, shine through this offering
we now return to you.
May our gifts and our very lives bless your world
and reveal your love.
In gratitude, we pray. Amen.

**GREAT THANKSGIVING** (*Luke 9, 2 Corinthians 3,*
*Transfiguration*)
> The Lord be with you.
>> **And also with you.**
> Lift up your hearts.
>> **We lift them up to God.**
> Let us give thanks to the Lord, our God.
>> **It is right to give God our thanks and praise.**

> It is right and a good and joyful thing,
>> always and everywhere, to give thanks to you,
>> Almighty God, creator of heaven and earth.
> From ancient times, you brought forth light
>> from primordial darkness,
>> created us in your image,
>> called us to be your people,
>> and shone through us with your love.
> When we wandered in darkness
>> and became lost in grumbling and fear,
>> you led us as a pillar of light
>> and beckoned us home.
> In the words of prophets and poets,
>> you called us to return to your light,
>> offering us a vision of renewal
>> and promising us a better future.
> And in the fullness of time, you sent your Son,
>> Christ Jesus, the Light of the World,
>> to redeem us with love and grace,
>> invite us to walk in the light,
>> and shine as light for the world.

> And so, with your people on earth,
>> and all the company of heaven,
>> we praise your name and join their unending hymn:

**Holy, holy, holy Lord, God of power and might,
heaven and earth are full of your glory.
Hosanna in the highest. Blessed is the one
who comes in the name of the Lord.
Hosanna in the highest.**

Holy are you, and blessed is your child of light,
Christ Jesus.
With humble gratitude, we remember the night
when the darkness of impending death
began closing in.
Jesus took the bread, blessed and broke it,
and gave it to disciples, who had witnessed
the glory of his transfiguration
and who would soon witness his death, saying:
"Take, eat, this is my body, given for you.
Do this in remembrance of me."
After supper, Jesus took the cup, blessed it
and gave it to his disciples, saying:
"Drink from this, all of you.
This is my life,
poured out for you and for many,
for the forgiveness of sins.
Do this, as often as your drink it,
in remembrance of me."

And so, in remembrance of these,
your mighty acts of love and light,
we offer ourselves in praise and thanksgiving.
As your covenant people
and as reflections of your glory,
in union with Christ's love for us,
we proclaim the mystery of faith.
**Christ has died.
Christ is risen.
Christ will come again.**

*PRAYER OF CONSECRATION*
Pour out your Holy Spirit on us
and on these gifts of bread and wine.
May these be for us your life and love,
shining through us with the power
of your Holy Spirit.
Through these gifts, may all be one with you,
one with each other, and one in the ministry
of love and light to the world,
until Christ comes in final victory
and we feast at your heavenly banquet.
Through Jesus Christ,
with the Holy Spirit in your holy Church,
all honor and glory is yours, Almighty God,
now and forevermore.
**Amen.**

# SENDING FORTH

*BENEDICTION (2 Corinthians 3, Luke 9)*
Go forth to shine with God's light and love.
**We'll shine joyously for all to see.**

Notes

# March 5, 2025

## Ash Wednesday

### B. J. Beu
*Copyright © B. J. Beu*

## COLOR

Purple

## SCRIPTURE READINGS

Joel 2:1-2, 12-17; Psalm 51:1-17; 2 Corinthians 5:20b–6:10;
Matthew 6:1-6, 16-21

## THEME IDEAS

Ash Wednesday begins the forty-day journey of Lent—
the journey where we follow Jesus' steps to Jerusalem
and, ultimately, the cross. Ash Wednesday invites us
onto a journey of introspection, where we reflect on
what it means to be a Christian, what it means to take up
one's cross, and what it means and to truly follow Jesus.
The imposition of ashes on our foreheads reminds us of
the frailty of our lives here on earth. We were created
out of the dust of the earth, and to dust we shall return.
Even with divine judgment at hand, God's mercy calls
us to begin our journeys anew, that we might be blessed
in Christ.

# INVITATION AND GATHERING

*CENTERING WORDS (Joel 2, Psalm 51)*
God's judgment nears. Yet even now, God yearns to remove the funeral shrouds we have woven for ourselves. The Lord is here, offering us the chance to begin again.

*CALL TO WORSHIP (Joel 2, Psalm 51)*
Blow the trumpet in Zion!
**Sound the alarm on God's holy mountain!**
The day of the Lord draws near.
**A day of darkness and gloom.**
Yet even now, God yearns to turn calamity into joy.
**We will return to the Lord.**
Leave behind the ways that lead to death.
**We will rend our hearts, not our clothing.**
Have mercy on us, O God.
**Put a new and right spirit within us.**

~or~

*CALL TO WORSHIP (Joel 2:12)*
"Return to me!"
**Christ calls, and we listen.**
"Return to me!"
**Christ calls, and we respond.**
"Return to me!"
**Christ calls, and we return . . .**
**to life, to love, to God.**

*OPENING PRAYER (Joel 2, Psalm 51)*
Merciful God, open our hearts to your healing love.
Call us anew to amend our ways,
as we embark on this Lenten journey.
Walk with us and teach us your love,
that we might be signs of your grace.
With joyous hope, we pray. Amen.

# PROCLAMATION AND RESPONSE

## PRAYER OF YEARNING (Psalm 51)

Holy One, cleanse us of our shortcomings
>> when we turn away from your paths.
May we find truth in our inward being,
>> as we embrace your wisdom in our hearts.
In this season of Lent,
>> wash clean the thoughts in our hearts, O God,
>>> and put a new and right spirit within us.
Do not cast us away from your presence,
>> and do not take your Holy Spirit from us.
Amen.

## WORDS OF ASSURANCE (Joel 2)

God is compassionate, slow to anger
>> and quick to forgive our transgressions.
Rejoice in the One who abides in steadfast love
>> and blesses us with mercy and grace.

## PASSING THE PEACE OF CHRIST (Joel 2)

Throw off the garments of death and embrace the life that God offers us this day. Let us return to the Lord, with loving and grateful hearts, as we share the peace of Christ with one another.

## RESPONSE TO THE WORD (Joel 2)

Holy One, remind us of the frailty of our lives,
>> that we might live each day to the fullest.
May your word grow in our hearts,
>> that we may face our mistakes
>> and return to your ways.
Bless us as we follow your Son,
>> through the season of Lent.

*CALL TO PRAYER (Matthew 6)*
>Let us enter into silent prayer, as we seek the One who sees in secret and who rewards those who draw near with yearning hearts and receptive spirits.

# THANKSGIVING AND COMMUNION

*THANKSGIVING OVER THE ASHES*
>Eternal God, you created us from the dust of the earth,
>>and to dust we one day return.
>As we place these ashes on our foreheads,
>>draw us back to you.
>Bless us with your steadfast love,
>>for you are slow to anger
>>>and rejoice the lost are found. Amen.

*OFFERING PRAYER (Matthew 6)*
>Gracious God, receive these offerings
>>in the spirit of your Son,
>>>who taught us to watch our hearts.
>For where our hearts are,
>>there our treasure will be also.
>May our treasure be in you, Holy One,
>>and in the welfare of your world. Amen.

# SENDING FORTH

*BENEDICTION (Psalm 51)*
>Bathe in the steadfast love of God.
>Dedicate your hearts to the Holy One
>>during this season of Lent.
>Embrace the joy of your salvation
>>and go with God's blessing.

# Notes

# March 9, 2025

## First Sunday in Lent

### Mary Scifres
*Copyright © Mary Scifres*

## COLOR

Purple

## SCRIPTURE READINGS

Deuteronomy 26:1-11; Psalm 91:1-2, 9-16;
Romans 10:8b-13; Luke 4:1-13

## THEME IDEAS

These readings, on the First Sunday of Lent, invite us
to remember who we are and whose we are. No matter
the journey we take, God is our faithful companion and
guide. As many hymn writers have noted, God is the
One who's gotten us this far. The devil tempts Jesus to
both forget and reject his heritage, his identity, and his
trust in God. But Jesus stands firmly on his heritage, as
a child of God and as a member of the Hebrew people.
Like Moses before him, Jesus knows that the Holy Spirit, who led him to this wilderness, will also lead him
through the wilderness. This theme is echoed throughout the three related readings as well.

# INVITATION AND GATHERING

**CENTERING WORDS** *(Deuteronomy 26, Psalm 91, Luke 4)*
God is our refuge and strength, our companion and guide. Leaning into this truth helps us find our way through difficult seasons of our lives.

**CALL TO WORSHIP** *(Deuteronomy 26, Psalm 91, Luke 4)*
Welcome home, beloved children of God!
**Gathered in God's arms, we come to worship.**
Sheltered in God's love, we come to grow in love.
**Abiding in God, we seek solace and comfort.**
Even as God sends us on wilderness journeys,
**we trust that God is with us,**
**guiding and protecting our days.**

**OPENING PRAYER** *(Deuteronomy 26, Romans 10, Luke 4)*
Merciful God, your ways lead to life;
your light shines in our darkness.
The promises you made to our ancestors
continue to this day.
We too share the bounty of your blessings,
and the grace of eternal life in your name.
May we be worthy of our calling
and help others find their way. Amen.
*(B. J. Beu)*
*Copyright © B. J. Beu*

# PROCLAMATION AND RESPONSE

*PRAYER OF YEARNING (Deuteronomy 26, Psalm 91, Luke 4)*
> God of our weary years, lift us up and guide us forward,
>> when we are tired beyond words.
> Pour your grace into our souls,
>> when we give in to temptation
>>> and stray where we were never meant to go.
> Shepherding God, guide us back to you
>> and show us the path home.
> In hope and gratitude, we pray

*WORDS OF ASSURANCE (Romans 10)*
> All who call on God's name are saved.
> We can rest assured in this promise.
> Amen and amen.

*RESPONSE TO THE WORD (Psalm 91)*
> In God's love, we are delivered.
> **In God's presence, we are sheltered.**
> In times of trouble and times of joy,
> **God is with us, always and everywhere.**

# THANKSGIVING AND COMMUNION

*INVITATION TO THE OFFERING (Deuteronomy 26)*
> As the ancient Hebrews were called to offer the first fruit of the harvest, so we are called to offer our gifts of gratitude to God. May God move in our hearts and minds, as we give generously, gratefully, and joyfully.

*OFFERING PRAYER (Deuteronomy 26)*
God of abundance, we offer these gifts,
    along with our praise and thanksgiving.
You generously pour out your love
    and the gifts of this good earth to us,
        each and every day.
Bless the gifts we return to you now,
    that they may bring abundant love and sustenance
        to many in need of your blessing.
With grateful hearts, we pray. Amen.

# SENDING FORTH

*BENEDICTION (Deuteronomy 26, Psalm 91, Luke 4)*
With God as our guide,
we go into the world.
With Christ as our companion,
**we go strengthened for the journey,**
and led with love.

# Notes

# March 16, 2025

## Second Sunday in Lent

### Mary Scifres
*Copyright © Mary Scifres*

## COLOR

Purple

## SCRIPTURE READINGS

Genesis 15:1-12, 17-18; Psalm 27; Philippians 3:17–4:1; Luke 13:31-35

## THEME IDEAS

Courage and the call to stand firm hold today's readings together. Abraham's doubts, the psalmist's fears, and even Jesus' frustration with Jerusalem's rejection, are all met with God's confidence and assurance that God's promises will be fulfilled. Paul echoes this message in his letter to the Philippians, as he calls them to "stand firm in the Lord," even when enemies are all around.

## INVITATION AND GATHERING

*CENTERING WORDS (Psalm 27, Philippians 4)*
Stand firm in the Lord. God's love is a mighty fortress of strength and grace.

*CALL TO WORSHIP (Psalm 27)*

God, our light and our salvation, calls us to worship.
**We gather in faith, confidence, and praise.**
Come; seek the face of God.
**God's face shines upon us with grace and love.**
Be strong, my friends, for God is here.
**Thanks be to God for this wonderful gift.**

*OPENING PRAYER (Genesis 15, Psalm 27, Philippians 3, Philippians 4)*

Mighty God, we come into your presence
    from many different places and situations.
Light our way in this time of worship.
Calm our hearts, focus our thoughts,
    and strengthen our faith,
        as we pray and praise this day. Amen.

# PROCLAMATION AND RESPONSE

*PRAYER OF YEARNING (Genesis 15, Psalm 27, Philippians 4, Luke 13)*

Mothering God, we often feel scattered and lost,
    separated from you and from one another.
Gather us in.
Comfort us in our loneliness.
Dispel our fears.
Correct our wayward feet and strengthen our faith,
    that we might hear your voice, trust your promises,
        and stand firm in your ways.
In your light and love, we pray. Amen.

*WORDS OF ASSURANCE (Psalm 27, Philippians 3, Philippians 4)*

Be strong and take heart.
God is with us here and now.
Christ's love is saving us, now and always.

## PASSING THE PEACE OF CHRIST (Psalm 27, Philippians 3, Philippians 4)

Sisters and brothers, we are light for one another, even as Christ is light for each of us. Let's share signs of Christ's light and love, as we pass the peace with one another.

## RESPONSE TO THE WORD or BENEDICTION (Psalm 27, Philippians 4, Luke 13)

God is our light and our salvation.
**We need not fear.**
Christ is the stronghold of our life.
**We need not be afraid.**
When evil scatters us to the winds,
**Christ gathers us with love and grace.**
Be strong, beloved ones.
**We are not alone.**
We are beloved children of God.
**We are sent with the Spirit's power
to love as we are loved.**

# THANKSGIVING AND COMMUNION

## INVITATION TO THE OFFERING (Genesis 15)

As the ancients brought goats and doves to honor and bless God, we are invited to bring our gifts of earthly treasure to honor and bless God. Whether we offer coins or dollars, checks or electronic donations, all gifts honor and bless God. Knowing this, may we share our treasure as generously with God as God has shared earthly treasure with us.

**OFFERING PRAYER** *(Genesis 15, Philippians 4)*
    Mighty God, bless these gifts,
        that they might bring strength to our faith,
        love to your world,
            and comfort to the forsaken.
    In your holy name, we pray. Amen.

# SENDING FORTH

**BENEDICTION** *(Psalm 27, Luke 13)*
    Be strong and take heart.
    God goes before us on the road of life.
    Go as beloved children of God.
    We will bring love to all of God's children.

**Notes**

# March 23, 2025

## Third Sunday in Lent

### B. J. Beu
*Copyright © B. J. Beu*

## COLOR

Purple

## SCRIPTURE READINGS

Isaiah 55:1-9; Psalm 63:1-8; 1 Corinthians 10:1-13;
Luke 13:1-9

## THEME IDEAS

God offers us water to drink, the bread of life, and the
sweet wine of salvation—all without price. Yet, we often
seek food and drink that does not satisfy. Though God
made an everlasting covenant with David, the unrigh-
teous are still called to change their ways. And woe to us
if we too quickly count ourselves among the righteous!
This third Sunday in Lent makes it clear that we must
repent or perish. Jesus' parable of the fig tree echoes
Isaiah's challenge, "Let the wicked forsake their ways"
(Luke 13:7). Paul warns that our ancestors ate spiritual
food and perished, for they strayed from God's paths.
We are called to repent and embrace God's abundant
life.

## INVITATION AND GATHERING

*CENTERING WORDS (Psalm 63)*
Seek God and thirst for the Lord. For God's steadfast love is sweet than honey and more satisfying that the finest bread.

*CALL TO WORSHIP (Isaiah 55, Psalm 63)*
The table is set. The banquet is laid.
**Our souls hunger and thirst for God.**
Our gracious host welcomes us here.
**God's steadfast love is better than life.**
Sing for joy in the shadow of God's wings.
**We have come to praise the living God.**

*OPENING PRAYER (Isaiah 55, Psalm 63, 1 Corinthians 10)*
Lord of overflowing abundance,
    we praise you with joyful lips
        and bless you with uplifted hands.
When our souls are parched,
    you offer us wine and milk without price
        and satisfy our hunger.
Guard us when we stand for what is right,
    and save us from the time of trial,
        that we may be worthy disciples of your Son,
           our rock and our redeemer. Amen.

## PROCLAMATION AND RESPONSE

*PRAYER OF YEARING (Isaiah 55, Psalm 63)*
Merciful God, when we suffer thirst,
    you refresh us with the waters of life.
When we set our jaws and lose our cool,
    you heal our hardness of heart.
Help us abide in your steadfast love,
    both now and forevermore. Amen.

*WORDS OF ASSURANCE (1 Corinthians 10, Luke 13)*
    God is our help in times of trial
        and when we lose our way.
    When we place our trust in Christ,
        God helps us stand and restores our honor.

*PASSING THE PEACE OF CHRIST (Isaiah 55, Psalm 63)*
    The Lord offers us everything we need without price.
    In celebration of this great gift, let us share our joy by
    passing the peace of Christ with one another.

*RESPONSE TO THE WORD (Isaiah 55)*
    Seek the Lord while God may be found.
    Call upon the Lord while God is near.
    Trust the One who abounds in steadfast love.

# THANKSGIVING AND COMMUNION

*OFFERING PRAYER (Luke 13)*
    Loving God, you have set the table before us
        and given us every good thing.
    In gratitude for your kindness and mercy,
        receive our gifts and our offerings.
    Accept our hearts into your keeping,
        that our lives may bear good fruit
            and that we may enter into your glory. Amen.

# SENDING FORTH

*BENEDICTION (Isaiah 55, Psalm 63)*
    Seek the Lord while God may be found.
        **We will call upon the Lord, while God is near.**
    Embrace the paths that lead to life.
        **We will return to our God.**
    Seek the Lord while God may be found.
        **We will call upon the Lord, while God is near.**

# Notes

# March 30, 2025

## Fourth Sunday in Lent

### Mary Scifres
*Copyright © Mary Scifres*

## COLOR

Purple

## SCRIPTURE READINGS

Joshua 5:9-12; Psalm 32; 2 Corinthians 5:16-21;
Luke 15:1-3, 11b-32

## THEME IDEAS

New beginnings and the invitation to embrace ourselves
as new creations flow through today's readings. As Joshua and the Israelites arrive in the land of Canaan, their
story, as God's people, begins anew. They are no longer
wandering in the wilderness, but have crossed into the
Promised Land. Similarly, the younger son in Jesus' parable of Luke 15 is transformed when he returns home to
find forgiveness and grace. Such gifts not only restore,
but exalt him. Paul invites us to embrace this invitation
and become new creations in Christ's forgiveness and
grace.

# INVITATION AND GATHERING

**CENTERING WORDS (*Joshua 5, Psalm 32, 2 Corinthians 5, Luke 15*)**
> Rejoice and be glad. In Christ, we are made new. In God, steadfast love guides us home.

**CALL TO WORSHIP (*2 Corinthians 5, Luke 15*)**
> Come, all ye faithful . . .
>> **to worship, praise, and pray.**
>
> Come, all ye unfaithful . . .
>> **for God's love welcomes us home.**
>
> Come into the presence of Christ . . .
>> **for Christ's grace makes us new and whole.**

**OPENING PRAYER (*Joshua 5, Luke 15*)**
> God of ages past and present faithfulness,
>> welcome us into your love,
>>> as we worship you this day.
>
> Draw closer to us,
>> that we might trust your promises
>> and follow your ways.
>
> In hope and faith, we pray. Amen.

# PROCLAMATION AND RESPONSE

**PRAYER OF YEARNING (*2 Corinthians 5, Luke 15*)**
> Father-Mother God, welcome us home
>> when we wander afar.
>
> Restore us with your compassion and love.
> Transform us with your miraculous grace,
>> that we might become the new creations
>> you envision us to be.

Strengthen us with the power of your Holy Spirit,
    that we might offer others
        the same welcome, grace, and love
           that you have offered us.
In your beloved name, we pray. Amen.

## WORDS OF ASSURANCE (2 Corinthians 5)

Everything old has passed away.
In Christ, you are a new creation,
    full of mercy and grace.
**In Christ, you are a new creation,**
    **full of mercy and grace.**

## PASSING THE PEACE OF CHRIST (2 Corinthians 5, Luke 15)

Reconciled to God through the grace of Christ, let's offer signs of reconciliation and love, as we share the peace of Christ.

## RESPONSE TO THE WORD (2 Corinthians 5)

Once, we only saw one another
from a human point of view.
    **Now, Christ invites us to see one another**
    **from a new vantage point.**
Look around. Look deeply. Look within.
What do you see?
    **We are ambassadors of Christ,**
    **seeing one another as new creations in God.**

*(Consider closing this time of response with a soloist singing "What a Wonderful World.")*

# THANKSGIVING AND COMMUNION

**INVITATION TO THE OFFERING (*Joshua 5,*
*2 Corinthians 5*)**
> In gratitude for all that God has done for us and as faithful disciples of Jesus Christ, let us share our gifts with God and God's world.

**OFFERING PRAYER (*Psalm 32, 2 Corinthians 5, Luke 15*)**
> With glad hearts, we offer these gifts to you, O God.
> Transform them with the power of your Holy Spirit,
> > that these gifts may bring forth new life.
> May our offering transform others' lives
> > into the new creation you promise to all. Amen.

# SENDING FORTH

**BENEDICTION (*scripture references*)**
> Created anew in Christ,
> > **we go to proclaim new life to the world.**
> Transformed by God's love and grace,
> > **we go to bring love and grace to all.**

# April 6, 2025

## Fifth Sunday in Lent

Rebecca Gaudino

## COLOR

Purple

## SCRIPTURE READINGS

Isaiah 43:16-21; Psalm 126; Philippians 3:4b-14;
John 12:1-8

## THEME IDEAS (Psalm 126; John 12)

John tells a story of how God has restored the fortune
(Ps. 126:1) of the Bethany family. Lazarus is alive, and he
sits at the table, eating and laughing with Jesus and his
disciples. No wonder Mary bought costly perfume to
pour on Jesus' feet! The last time she knelt at Jesus' feet,
she shared her devastation that Jesus had not arrived in
time to save her brother (John 11:32). Now she kneels at
Jesus' feet and washes them in gratitude and love. Like
the perfume of nard, her care for Jesus fills the entire
house with fragrance. Less than a week later, Jesus will
wash his disciples' feet and teach what he experienced
in Mary's example. What do love and discipleship look
like? Sometimes just the simplest acts of welcome, caring, and comfort: for Jesus, for the poor, for everyone. In

this act of celebration, Mary unknowingly foreshadows the next difficult steps in Jesus' life—his journey to the cross. But Jesus will walk with feet perfumed by love.

# INVITATION AND GATHERING

*CENTERING WORDS (Psalm 126)*
God turns our tears to shouts of joy. Christ turns our weeping into laughter.

*CALL TO WORSHIP (Psalm 126)*
When we have been hurt and lost,
**God brings us laughter and joy.**
When our lives reach a dead end,
**God opens a way forward.**
When the rivers of our lives drys up,
**God sends living water to quench our thirst.**
God has done great things for us!
**Let us rejoice!**

*OPENING PRAYER (Psalm 126, John 12)*
God of Love, you know our lives inside and out—
the times of joy and laughter,
and the times of loss and pain.
You accompanied our ancestors of faith into exile
and then journeyed with them
back to the Promised Land.
Jesus our sibling, you wept at the grave of Lazarus
and then you celebrated at the dinner table
with your resurrected friend.
Be with us in times of plenty and times of want,
and let us rejoice in your presence,
for you see us and care for us.
In the name of the Embracing Spirit, we pray. Amen.

# PROCLAMATION AND RESPONSE

**PRAYER OF YEARNING (Psalm 126, John 12)**
> Compassionate God,
>> we do not always see the harvest of joy
>>> that we sow from our tears.
> Some losses take hold of us
>> and we dwell in disappointment and grief.
> We don't always know what to think of you.
> We want to embrace new life, hope, and joy,
>> but don't always know how.
> Bless us with your merciful help,
>> that we might walk from our tombs like Lazarus,
>>> and sit by Jesus' side, eating and laughing.
> Help us kneel at Jesus' feet in love and commitment,
>> as we celebrate our new lives.
> Come to us, healing God,
>> and renew us and our love for you. Amen.

**WORDS OF ASSURANCE (Psalm 126)**
> God promises to do great things for us.
> God comforts us and brings us with new life.
> Blessed are you, our God of compassion and hope.
> Amen.

**INTRODUCTION TO THE WORD (John 12)**
> Today we hear the story of a woman who has known grief and joy. She has wept at the death of her brother Lazarus, and now he sits at the family table, alive and well. Imagine her relief, her joy, her amazement at this turn of events. This is all because of another much-loved man who sits before her, Jesus. How can she ever repay him? How can she ever let him know the depth of her gratitude, the depth of her faith?

**RESPONSE TO THE WORD (Psalm 126, John 12)**
　　Restore our fortunes too, O God!
　　Fill our mouths with laughter.
　　May we kneel at Jesus' feet in thanksgiving and love.
　　As disciples made new, may we walk with him
　　　　on the path to Jerusalem with our love. Amen.

*(Think about how you can bring the idea of fragrance into your worship experience. Is incense a possibility? Or think about choosing two or three fragrances, nothing overpowering, and put a small amount on a slip of paper, color-coded for the fragrances—green for pine fragrance, etc. Have people come forward and choose one of these slips of paper to take with them for the week. Ask them to put this slip of paper beside their favorite chair and think of something they can thank God for. How can they show their love for God?)*

# THANKSGIVING AND COMMUNION

**INVITATION TO THE OFFERING (Psalm 126, John 12)**
　　Let us share our gifts from our deep gratitude to Jesus, our savior, who answers our sorrow with joy and our tears with comfort. Let us share our gifts out of thanksgiving to God and out of love for the world.

**OFFERING PRAYER (Psalm 126, John 12)**
　　Dearest Friend, you chose a path of suffering
　　　　to reach out to us in our suffering.
　　Use us and our gifts to extend your love and comfort
　　　　to reach people in places of loss and grief.
　　Use us and our gifts this day
　　　　to bring hope and compassion to those who weep,
　　　　　　that they may know your miraculous power
　　　　　　　　and your fullness of life.
　　Use us and our gifts to bring shouts of joy
　　　　to those who weep with bitter tears. Amen.

# SENDING FORTH

**BENEDICTION (Psalm 126, John 12)**
Jesus left the house of Mary, Martha, and Lazarus
on his way to Jerusalem.
**Jesus left this house of comfort and friendship,**
**knowing the deep love of his disciple Mary.**
So let us leave this house of peace today,
knowing we will meet Jesus in Jerusalem soon.
**And while we travel from here to there,**
**May we carry fragrant love for our brother,**
**savior, and beloved friend. Amen.**

Notes

# April 13, 2025

## Palm/Passion Sunday

### B. J. Beu
*Copyright © B. J. Beu*

## COLOR

Purple

## PALM SUNDAY READINGS

Psalm 118:1-2, 19-29; Luke 19:28-40

## PASSION SUNDAY READINGS

Isaiah 50:4-9a; Psalm 31:9-16; Philippians 2:5-11;
Luke 22:14–23:56

## THEME IDEAS

After the initial joy when Jesus entered Jerusalem to loud hosannas, fickleness of heart and betrayal follow closely behind. Shortly after singing Jesus' praises, as he rode a colt into the holy city, the crowds (and even his own disciples) betrayed and denied him. To avoid moving from the joy of Palm Sunday to the joy of Easter, today's service focuses on the all too human trait of falling away.

# INVITATION AND GATHERING

*CENTERING WORDS (Psalm 118, Luke 19)*
Blessed is the one who comes in the name of the Lord.

*CALL TO WORSHIP (Psalm 118)*
Jesus is the rock of our salvation.
**But the builders rejected that rock.**
Jesus is the gate of righteousness.
**But so many consider him a fraud.**
Jesus has become the cornerstone of our lives.
**Shall we enter his gate of righteousness?**
Yes! Let us worship the Lord.

~or~

*CALL TO WORSHIP (Psalm 118, Luke 19)*
*(Begin service with a bare altar/Lord's Table. The italicized words are read offstage.)*

When they had come near Bethphage and Bethany,
at the place called the Mount of Olives,
Jesus sent two of his disciples ahead, saying:
*"Go into the village ahead of you, and as you enter it*
*you will find tied there a colt that has never been ridden.*
*Untie it and bring it here. If anyone asks you, 'Why are*
*you untying it?' just say this,*
*'The Lord has need of it.'"*
**This is the day that the Lord has made.**
**Let us rejoice and be glad in it.**

*(Church bell, chime, or gong sounds. Have youth come forward and cover the altar with brightly colored cloth as the words below are read.)*

After bringing the colt to Jesus
and throwing their cloaks on its back,
the disciples set Jesus upon it.
As he road along, people spread their cloaks
upon the road.
    **The stone that the builders rejected**
    **has become the chief cornerstone.**
    **This is the Lord's doing.**
    **It is marvelous in our eyes.**

*(Church bell, chime, or gong sounds.)*

Open the gates of righteousness, O God,
that we may enter through them.
    **This is the day that the Lord has made.**
    **Let us rejoice and be glad in it.**

*(Begin light, joyful music underneath. If you have liturgical dancers, dance a single Christ Candle or multiple lights as the words below are read.)*

The Lord is God, and God has given us light
as a lamp to our feet.
    **The light shines in the darkness,**
    **and the darkness has not overcome it.**

*(Church bell, chime, or gong sounds as music continue to play.)*

Bind the festival procession with palm branches.
Enter the gates of righteousness with shouts
of thanksgiving.
    **Blessed is the one who comes**
    **in the name of the Lord.**
    **Peace in heaven,**
    **and glory to God in the highest heaven!**

Hearing the crowd's shouts of praise,
some of the Pharisees said to Jesus,
"Teacher, order your disciples to stop."

*(Music stops abruptly at word, "stop.")*

But Jesus answered,
  *"I tell you, if these were silent,
  the stones would shout out."*

*(Blow a low horn or play an instrument that evokes the sound
of stones crying out.)*

This is the day that the Lord has made.
  **Let us rejoice and be glad in it!**

*(Youth enter and march around the sanctuary to "All Glory,
Laud and Honor" or similar song.)*

## OPENING PRAYER (Luke 22-23, Philippians 2)
Foundation of our faith,
  your Son humbled himself on the back of a colt.
Then he entered Jerusalem in lowly estate
  to bring joy to the hearts of children.
Forsaking his place at your side,
  Jesus emptied himself of prestige and power
    to become a servant to all.
On this day of joy and remembrance,
  sing in our hearts once more,
    that we too may dance with the children—
      for to such belong the kingdom of heaven.
Amen.

# PROCLAMATION AND RESPONSE

*PRAYER OF YEARNING (Philippians 2, Luke 22-23)*
Abiding Spirit, your love meets us in our need.
On this Palm Sunday celebration,
    we yearn to be free of doubt
        healed of our weaknesses,
           and freed from our denials and betrayals.
Correct our wayward feet and our fickle hearts,
    for we long to walk in your ways,
        lest we stumble and fall in times of trial.
In your holy name, we pray. Amen.

~or~

*PRAYER OF YEARNING (Luke 22-23)*
God of righteousness,
    draw near to us in coming week.
We yearn to keep singing our hosannas,
    but fear that we too may lose our convictions
        in the face of an angry mob.
We long to see ourselves as your champions,
    but fear that we too might deny you
        or betray you with a kiss.
Strengthen our resolve during Holy Week,
    that we may remain your faithful disciples. Amen.

*WORDS OF ASSURANCE (Psalm 118)*
Christ has opened the gates of righteousness
    and beckons us to walk through.
The stone that the builders rejected
    has become the cornerstone of our salvation.

*RESPONSE TO THE WORD (Isaiah 50, Luke 22–23)*
Merciful God, your words sustain the weary
and awaken those who slumber.
Put your words of life in our hearts,
that we may be strengthened to walk with Christ
until the bitter end. Amen.

*CALL TO PRAYER (Psalm 31)*
Like broken vessels, we need God's healing.
Like those who are dead,
we need God's Spirit to quicken us.
Like a city under siege,
we need God's protection and deliverance.
God, you are the one who delivers us from evil,
helps us stand in times of trial,
and makes us whole again. Amen.

# THANKSGIVING AND COMMUNION

*OFFERING PRAYER (Philippians 2, Luke 22-23)*
We thank you, O God, for your generous Spirit
We praise you for Christ's gift of self,
and your never-failing love.
For your many gifts,
we thank you.
For walking with us in our weakness,
we praise you.
Receive these gifts in token and thanks
for the love you offer us—
a love that makes us well and whole. Amen.

# SENDING FORTH

*BENEDICTION (Psalm 118)*
On the back of a donkey,
   **Jesus came to bless us.**
With the light of his love,
   **Jesus came to illumine our way.**
From the power of aimlessness and sin,
   **Jesus came to set us free.**
With the power of the Holy Spirit,
   **Jesus came to save us.**
Go with the blessings of God's anointed.

~or~

*BENEDICTION (Psalm 118)*
This is the day that the Lord has made.
As we go forth from this place,
   let us rejoice and be glad in it!

Notes

# April 17, 2025

## Holy Thursday

### Leigh Ann Shaw

## COLOR

Purple

## SCRIPTURE READINGS

Exodus 12:1-4, (5-10), 11-14; Psalm 116:1-4, 12-19;
1 Corinthians 11:23-26; John 13:1-17, 31b-35

## THEME IDEAS

Every vignette for this moment touches our human senses. Exodus' Passover meal remembers God telling Moses to use lamb, bread, and bitter herbs. The Corinthian passage passes on the teachings of Jesus' last meal. Jesus' meal is meant to be lived, remembered, and repeated by those who remain after he is gone. The Gospel of John tells of the betrayal of Jesus, how Jesus washed Peter's feet, and offers a new commandment of love. It is service, hospitality, and the beautiful intimacy between God and humanity that frame these Holy moments. Those who follow Jesus are challenged to embody faith through hearing, seeing, feeling, tasting, and smelling the good news.

# INVITATION AND GATHERING

### CENTERING WORDS (John 13)

The table is near, our seats assigned. Jesus shares this moment with us. His grace calls for love, but are we ready to take our place?

### CALL TO WORSHIP (1 Corinthians 11, John 13)

Come to this moment; God's love is before us.
**We heed the summons that calls us to this time.**
Wash your hands; God will wash your feet.
**How do we prepare to receive Christ's love?**
With humble acceptance of God's grace,
**turn and receive the gifts that are offered.**
We are ready partake of the gifts of the divine.

# PROCLAMATION AND RESPONSE

### PRAYER OF YEARNING (John 13)

Holy God, when our faith is small and impatient,
overcome our reluctance to receive your grace.
When we expect hurt and hate,
help us endure the trials of living.
Open our eyes to behold Jesus's life-giving gifts,
that we might no longer guard our hearts
from the pain that the world brings.
Like Peter before us, meet us in our weakness
when we walk away, deny love,
even fail to receive the meal of our Lord. Amen.

### WORDS OF ASSURANCE

Even as we wander and fail to come before Christ,
God offers us love.
Do not fear but come to the table of grace.
All are welcomed here.

*PASSING OF THE PEACE (John 13)*
> Let us share the gift of forgiveness and God's love with our neighbors. Let us exchange signs of Christ's peace.

*RESPONSE TO THE WORD (John 13)*
> God has been glorified. Christ is with us
> and calls us to love one another.
> **We will love one another**
> **as Christ has commanded us.**

# THANKSGIVING AND COMMUNION

*INVITATION TO THE OFFERING (John 13)*
> This is our time to respond to the Word of God. God offers mercy where there is injustice. God offers life for the broken. We are not called servants, but friends through the grace of the God. Let us make our humble offering in response the many gifts we have received from our Holy God.

*OFFERING PRAYER*
> God of unrelenting mercy, use today's offering
> to bless your creation.
> Use our lives to heal our communities.
> Let all we have offered, in heart and hand,
> bring joy and faith to your world. Amen.

*INVITATION TO COMMUNION (1 Corinthians 11:23-26)*
> Come to the table! This is the table of remembrance.
> This is the table of Grace. Do not fear,
> but release the distractions of your mind
> and remember the offering of God.

> Let our hearts be joined in prayer.

95

We remember the stories of miraculous feeding—
    manna and bread, fishes and loaves and wine.
We ask your blessing, Holy One,
    upon these common elements of bread and juice.
You feed us in ways that go far beyond
    our understanding.
Through the awesome wonders of creation
    to the joy of human love,
        you have blessed us.
You became present to us in Jesus, who walked with us,
    was denied, betrayed, and still called us to love.
You remain present to us in the working
    of your Holy Spirit.
We give thanks for all the ways you assure us
    of your steadfast nature.

Jesus, Lamb of God, gathered for a meal
    with the family of disciples.
He took the bread, offered gratitude for it,
    broke it, and shared it, saying:
        "Do this in remembrance of me."
After the meal, Jesus took the common cup,
    offered gratitude to God, and said:
        "This cup is the new covenant.
        Drink it in remembrance of me."

Whoever eats this bread and drinks from this cup,
    in memory of Jesus, will share in life eternal.
All are welcome who sincerely desire to know the Lord
    and wish to receive God's blessing.
Let all come forward to the table.

# SENDING FORTH

***BENEDICTION***
>We have been made clean,
>>as we've feasted on the Word
>>and received the meal of Christ's table.
>
>In humility, go out now, aware of what is to come.
>Go forth, overflowing with appreciation and love.
>Amen.

Notes

# April 18, 2025

## Good Friday

### Mary Scifres
*Copyright © Mary Scifres*

## COLOR

Black or None

## SCRIPTURE READINGS

Isaiah 52:13–53:12; Psalm 22; Hebrews 10:16-25;
John 18:1–19:42

## THEME IDEAS

The scriptures for this mournful day elicit themes of
great sorrow: death, loneliness, suffering, and evil. The
theme of sacrifice, that arises as we reflect on Jesus'
death on the cross, reminds us that even the sorrows of
this day are incomparable to the great love of God.

# INVITATION AND GATHERING

**CENTERING WORDS** *(John 18, John 19)*
Come, children of God, and hear the story of Jesus' trial
and death. Listen and know that God loves you.

**CALL TO WORSHIP** *(Isaiah 53, Psalm 22, John 18, John 19)*

On this holy day of remembrance,
we mourn the death of our Lord, Jesus Christ.
**We remember Christ's love.**
On this holy day of sorrow,
we grieve the ways we cause God pain.
**We remember Christ's suffering.**
On this holy day of grief,
we acknowledge what must die within
to follow Christ.
**We remember Christ's teachings.**
On this holy day of reflection,
we listen for God's voice.
**We will open our ears to hear,
even in the silence of this day.**

**OPENING PRAYER** *(Isaiah 53, Psalm 22)*

Elusive One, where do you hide when grief and pain
    shroud us in darkness and mist?
Where do you go when all hope fades
    in the dying of the light?
How can we bear the excruciating emptiness
    of your absence.
Your ways are beyond us, mysterious One,
    cloaking us like a funeral shroud.
Be with us when all lights go out.
Be near us, even when we deny and betray you. Amen.
*(B. J. Beu)*
*Copyright © B. J. Beu*

# PROCLAMATION AND RESPONSE

*CALL TO CONFESSION (Hebrews 10)*
> Approach God with a true heart.
> Come before Christ with faith in God's mercy.
> Surely Christ, who is faithful and merciful,
>> will hear our prayers.

*PRAYER OF CONFESSION (Hebrews 10)*
> Merciful God, we do not always listen
>> when you speak your law in our thoughts.
> We do not always live the love
>> you have written on our hearts.
> We fear that your mercy has limits
>> and doubt the assurance of your forgiveness.
> Forgive our timid minds, our hardened hearts,
>> and our unfounded fears.
> Fill us with your mercy,
>> that we might love you and others
>>> with all our hearts, minds, souls, and strength.
> Amen.

*WORDS OF ASSURANCE (Hebrews 10)*
> God has made a covenant through Christ Jesus—
>> a covenant of love and mercy,
>> a covenant of forgiveness and reconciliation,
>> a covenant of and death and rebirth.
> Accept God's mercy.
> Let Christ's love refresh your spirit.
> Hold fast to the hope we have in Christ Jesus. Amen.

*RESPONSE TO THE WORD (John 18, Matthew 6, Luke 11)*
> Christ Jesus, we know that your kingdom
>> is not from this world.
>> **We pray that your kingdom might come on earth
>> as it is in heaven.**

You came to testify to the truth.
**We pray that your will might be done on earth
as it is in heaven.**
You claim us and call us to abide in your truth.
**Forgive us our sins, as we forgive those
who sin against us.**
We know that you did not come for worldly glory.
**But all honor and glory is yours, Christ Jesus,
now and forevermore. Amen.**

# THANKSGIVING AND COMMUNION

**OFFERING PRAYER** *(Isaiah 52, Isaiah 53, Hebrew 10)*
Christ Jesus, you have given us so much.
Even as we grieve your death on the cross,
we are grateful for the beautiful life you led
and for your example of loving deeply
and living faithfully.
Bless the gifts of our lives and the gifts of our offering,
that we may help others experience your deep love
and that we may be an example
of faithful living. Amen.

# SENDING FORTH

**BENEDICTION** *(Hebrews 10)*
Remember this day and keep it holy.
Remember Christ's love and hold it in your hearts.
Remember Christ's sacrifice, and trust God's grace.
Amen.

# Notes

# April 20, 2025

## Easter Sunday

### Mary Petrina Boyd

## COLOR

White

## SCRIPTURE READINGS

Acts 10:34-43; Psalm 118:1-2, 14-24; 1 Corinthians 15:19-26; John 20:1-18 (or Luke 24:1-12)

## THEME IDEAS

Easter Sunday is the pinnacle of the Christian year, as we proclaim the triumph of life over death. The Easter gospel is the center of this day. In both Luke and John, those coming to the tomb expect death, but instead find new life. Those who first encountered the empty tomb were confused and terrified, but the living reality of Jesus astounded them and gave them joy.

# INVITATION AND GATHERING

**CENTERING WORDS** *(John 20, Luke 24)*
The stone is rolled away. The tomb is empty. Christ is risen!

~or~

**CENTERING WORDS** *(John 20, Luke 24)*
Instead of death, there is new life, rich and abundant!

**CALL TO WORSHIP** *(John 20, Luke 24)*
*(Quotes the hymn, "Christ the Lord is Risen Today." Follow by singing the hymn.)*
Christ the Lord is risen today.
**Alleluia! Alleluia!**
Earth and heaven in chorus say:
**Alleluia! Alleluia!**
Love's redeeming work is done.
**Alleluia! Alleluia!**
Christ has opened paradise.
**Alleluia! Alleluia!**

~or~

**CALL TO WORSHIP** *(Psalm 118, Acts 10)*
This is the day that the Lord has made.
**Let us rejoice and be glad in it!**
This is the day of resurrection.
**Let us rejoice and celebrate!**
This is Easter Sunday.
**Alleluia! Alleluia!**

**OPENING PRAYER** *(John 20, Luke 24)*
God of life and love, we are eager to hear the good news
of new life.
Enter our lives and cast our fears aside.
Lead us on a journey from grief and despair
to hope and joy.
We are ready to celebrate
and give thanks for your transforming love.
We are eager to rejoice in the glory of this day!
Give us Easter spirits and open hearts. Amen.

# PROCLAMATION AND RESPONSE

**PRAYER OF YEARNING** *(John 20, Luke 24)*
Come, O God, and bring new life
    to the dead places in our hearts.
When are weary and afraid,
    help us trust your never-failing love.
May this love banish our fears,
    nourish our spirits,
        and deepen our joy. Amen.

**WORDS OF ASSURANCE** *(Psalm 118)*
God's love is faithful and everlasting.
This is the day that God has made.
It is filled with new life and hope.

**PASSING THE PEACE OF CHRIST** *(Acts 10)*
The message of peace is good news through Jesus Christ!

**PRAYER OF PREPARATION** *(John 20, Luke 24)*
God of life and love, we are here this morning
    to hear the good news of Easter.
Cast aside our doubts and fears,
    that we may hear your deep truth of life.
Help us listen with expectation and hope. Amen.

**LITANY OR RESPONSE TO THE WORD** *(John 20)*
*(This is the essence of John's Easter story.)*
Woman, why are you crying?
    **They have taken away my Lord.**
Who are you looking for?
    **Tell me where you have taken him.**
Mary.
    **Rabbouni, Teacher!**
Go and tell what you have seen.
    **I have seen the Lord!**

## LITANY OR RESPONSE TO THE WORD (Luke 24)

*(This is Luke's Easter story in brief, told by the women who were there. It could be read by three or more women, each taking a line in turn.)*

Woman 1   We went to the tomb, bringing fragrant spices to anoint Jesus' body.

Woman 2   The stone was rolled away.

Woman 3   The body was gone.

Woman 1   Two men dressed in gleaming, bright clothing were there.

Woman 2   We were frightened. What was happening?

Woman 3   The men said, "Why do you look for the living among the dead? He isn't here but has risen!

Woman 1   We went home and told the disciples.

Woman 2   They didn't believe us. They thought we spoke nonsense.

Woman 3   Peter went to see for himself. He was amazed!

**ALL       Jesus is alive! Alleluia!**

## PRAYER OF RESPONSE (John 20, Luke 24)

Gracious God, thank you for life and hope,
> your gifts of Easter.
When death and evil seemed to rule the day,
> you brought forth life abundant.
Now, when we are afraid and discouraged,
> remind us that love is stronger than death.
Like spring flowers,
> your loving beauty is everywhere,
>> encouraging and renewing our spirits.
May we be Easter people
> and rejoice in your love. Amen.

# THANKSGIVING AND COMMUNION

*INVITATION TO THE OFFERING (Psalm 118)*
Let us rejoice and give thanks this day, bringing our gifts to God.

~or~

*INVITATION TO THE OFFERING (Psalm 118)*
God is good.
   **God's faithful love endures forever!**
God is our strength and protection.
   **God's gracious joy brightens our lives!**
Let us give thanks to God through our gifts!
   **We will rejoice and share God's bounty!**

*OFFERING PRAYER (John 20, Luke 24)*
God of life and love, we are grateful
      for your promise of resurrection and new life.
Your love is stronger than the powers of evil
      and injustice.
With joy, we bring our gifts to you this day.
Use our gifts and our lives to proclaim Christ's triumph
      over death. Amen

# SENDING FORTH

*BENEDICTION (John 20, Luke 24)*
We have heard the story.
Life triumphed over death.
Grief became joy.
Go now and tell the good news: Christ is risen!
Alleluia!

# Notes

# April 27, 2025

## Second Sunday of Easter

### Mary Scifres
*Copyright © Mary Scifres*

## COLOR

White

## SCRIPTURE READINGS

Acts 5:27-32; Psalm 150; Revelation 1:4-8; John 20:19-31

## THEME IDEAS

Miraculous faith is a common theme that flows through today's readings. The disciples trust their vision when Jesus appears in their midst after his death. Even doubting Thomas comes to not just believe, but to proclaim Jesus' divinity. The psalmist calls all of creation to praise the mighty God. John sings and prophesies to the glory of the Alpha and Omega, and Peter recounts the Great Mystery of Christ's death and resurrection. These common words of faith, that so frequently roll off of our tongues, proclaim miracles that are far from common. We are called to keep the mystery and miracle of Easter alive throughout the year and throughout our lives of faith.

# INVITATION AND GATHERING

**CENTERING WORDS** *(Acts 5, Psalm 150, Revelation 1, John 20)*

Let all creation proclaim and rejoice: Christ is risen. Overcoming death, he is the Alpha and Omega, the powerful beginning and end of all things, the one who is and was and is to come.

**CALL TO WORSHIP** *(Acts 5, Psalm 150, John 20)*

With trumpet sounds and singing hearts,
**we come to praise the Lord.**
As faithful witnesses of Christ's grace and love,
**we come to praise the Lord.**
Coming here with our doubts and our faith,
**we come to praise the Lord.**

**OPENING PRAYER** *(Acts 5, Psalm 150, Revelation 1, John 20)*

God of mystery and miracles,
breathe your peace upon us.
Reveal your presence,
as we look for you each day.
Strengthen our faith and our trust,
as we pray for miracles for one another
and for all of your creation. Amen.

# PROCLAMATION AND RESPONSE

**PRAYER OF YEARNING** *(John 20)*

Loving Christ, you welcomed Thomas' questions,
even his doubts.
Welcome us, too, with your grace and your love.
Offer your hand of forgiveness

and show us the truth of your presence.
Fill us with the power of your love,
  that your grace, forgiveness, and love
    may flow freely to others.
In gratitude and joy, we pray. Amen.

**WORDS OF ASSURANCE** *(Acts 5, John 20)*
In grace, we are forgiven.
In love, we are freed.
In Christ, peace and assurance are ours.

**PASSING THE PEACE OF CHRIST** *(John 20)*
Peace be with you.
  **And also with you.**
Share this peace with words and actions of love.

**RESPONSE TO THE WORD** *(Acts 5, John 20)*
Whether we doubt or believe,
  **the miracle of life is real.**
Whether we question or affirm,
  **the miracle of God's love is here.**
Whether we distrust or avow,
  **the miracle of Christ's Spirit**
  **makes us the body of Christ.**

# THANKSGIVING AND COMMUNION

**OFFERING PRAYER** *(Acts 5, John 20)*
Mighty God, pour out your Holy Spirit on these gifts.
Bless them with your miraculous power,
  that they may become mighty gifts
    of love, justice, and peace—
      gifts with the powers to heal our world.
In your holy name, we pray. Amen.

111

# SENDING FORTH

**BENEDICTION** *(Acts 5, John 20)*
Go forth as witnesses to the miracle of God's love.
**We go to bring the miracle of God's love
to the world.**

Notes

# May 4, 2025

## Third Sunday of Easter

### B. J. Beu
*Copyright © B. J. Beu*

## COLOR

White

## SCRIPTURE READINGS

Acts 9:1-6, (7-20); Psalm 30; Revelation 5:11-14; John 21:1-19

## THEME IDEAS

God's love rescues us in many ways. On the road to Damascus, Saul is rescued from himself—his desire to persecute the fledgling Christian community was to the detriment of his soul and against God's designs. The psalmist extols God's power to heal and save us from our foes. The Book of Revelation rejoices in the Lamb, who takes away the sins of the world. And the Gospel of John depicts Jesus taking away the shame of Peter's three public denials by requiring three public declarations of his love. Love rescues us and calls us to action: Saul to proclaim the gospel, Peter to feed his masters' sheep. Just as God rescues us from the pit, God calls us to follow Jesus.

# INVITATION AND GATHERING

**CENTERING WORDS** *(John 21, Revelation 5)*
The Lamb who sits on the throne of life calls us to feed
his sheep and love his little ones.

**CALL TO WORSHIP** *(Acts 9, Psalm 30)*
Great winds drive our spirits across the sky,
**opening our hearts to hope and joy.**
Unseen powers on high move in our lives,
**turning our mourning into dancing.**
Weeping may last the night,
**but joy comes with the morning.**

~or~

**CALL TO WORSHIP** *(Psalm 30, Revelation 5)*
Rejoice in the Lord.
**Praise God's holy name.**
Worthy is the Lamb of our praise.
**Worthy is the righteous one**
**of blessing, honor, and glory.**
Rejoice in the Lord.
**Praise God's holy name.**

**OPENING PRAYER** *(Acts 9, John 21)*
Lord of Life, you meet us on the road,
challenge our prejudices,
and upend of our lives.
Remove the scales from our eyes—
that we may see the breadth of your love,
the diversity of the ones we are called to love,
and the joy of extending your welcome.
Fill us with your Spirit,
that we might love one another
as our shepherd loves us. Amen.

# PROCLAMATION AND RESPONSE

*PRAYER OF YEARING (Acts 9, John 21)*
Merciful God, help us leave ignorance behind,
as we learn to love as you would have us love.
Heal our vision when false piety to blinds us,
as Saul before us.
Rescue us when we go astray,
and renew our desire to feed Christ's sheep
and to tend his lambs. Amen.

*WORDS OF ASSURANCE (Psalm 30)*
The time for weeping is over,
for joy comes with the morning.
Rejoice, people of God.
God's Spirit saves us,
even when we give up on ourselves.

*PASSING THE PEACE OF CHRIST (John 21, Revelation 5)*
The Lamb, who sits on the thrown, invites us to feed his
sheep and tend his lambs. Let us begin by turning to one
another and sharing signs of peace this morning.

*RESPONSE TO THE WORD or INVITATION TO THE
OFFERING (John 21)*
Christ asks: "Do you love me? Feed my lambs."
**Receive our love, Lord.**
Christ challenges: "Do you love me? Tend my sheep."
**Receive our service, Holy One.**
Christ entreats: "Do you love me? Feed my sheep."
**Receive our Gifts, gracious savior.**

# THANKSGIVING AND COMMUNION

**OFFERING PRAYER** *(Acts 9, Psalm 30, Revelation 5, John 21)*
>Great Spirit, receive the gifts from our hands this day.
>For you rescue us from ourselves
>>and free us to love others,
>>>as you have loved us.
>After a long slumber in ignorance and fear,
>>we offer you our gratitude
>>>for the joy that comes in the morning.
>Accept this offering, as a sign of our commitment,
>>to tend your sheep and feed your lambs. Amen.

# SENDING FORTH

**BENEDICTION** *(Revelation 5, John 21)*
>The Spirit blows us across the sky,
>>**showing us God's little ones.**
>The Lamb of God looks on us with love,
>>**calling us to feed God's sheep.**
>The Spirit leads us through the darkest nights
>>**to a joy that comes with the morning.**

# Notes

# May 11, 2025

## Fourth Sunday of Easter
## Festival of the Christian Home/
## Mother's Day

### Mary Scifres
*Copyright © Mary Scifres*

## COLOR

White

## SCRIPTURE READINGS

Acts 9:36-43; Psalm 23; Revelation 7:9-17; John 10:22-30

## THEME IDEAS

The dramatic miracle of Acts 9 (Peter raising Dorcas from death), and the glorious vision of Revelation 7 (the faithful before the thrown of God), create a contrast to the gentle scene many imagine when reading Psalm 23. Yet, even the psalmist speaks of the dark valley of death and the need for God's protection in a dangerous world. Death and danger are realities we face, even as Easter people. God promises to walk with us through those realities, caring for us as gently, and defending us as viciously, as the good shepherd does for his flock or any mother bear would for her cubs.

# INVITATION AND GATHERING

**CENTERING WORDS** *(Psalm 23, John 10)*
In this world of trials, tribulations, dangers, and death, our loving God watches over us, as a mother bear watches over her cubs. Our Lord walks with us, as a loving companion cares for her beloved. Our savior makes us lie down in green pastures, as a good shepherd cares for his sheep.

**CALL TO WORSHIP** *(Psalm 23, Revelation 7)*
The God of love and grace invites us in.
**Blessed be the God of love!**
The God of power and might welcomes us here.
**Glory to God on high!**
The God of wisdom and truth speaks to us now.
**Praise the One who speaks truth to our hearts!**

**OPENING PRAYER** *(Psalm 23, Revelation 7, John 10)*
Shepherding God, guide us in this time of worship.
Help us receive your wisdom
and respond with lives of faithful discipleship.
Walk closely with us
and help us feel your constant presence,
both now and forevermore. Amen.

# PROCLAMATION AND RESPONSE

**CALL TO PRAYER or INTRODUCTION TO THE WORD**
*(Psalm 23, John 10)*
The Shepherd of comfort gathers us in.
**We come, seeking welcome and love.**
**We stay, finding rest and renewal.**
In our prayer and reflection,
**may we discover these wonderful gifts from God.**

**PRAYER OF YEARNING (Acts 9, Psalm 23, Festival of the Christian Home)**
> God of love and grace, we yearn for a world
>> where love and grace guide our steps
>>> and bless our days.
> We dream of families and communities
>> led by love and guided by grace.
> Yet, division, danger, and death
>> interrupt our dreams and dampen our hopes
>>> for our lives.
> Comfort us in our sorrow.
> Heal us in our troubles.
> Protect us in this dangerous world.
> Unify us with your love and grace,
>> that we might offer your abundant love
>>> and amazing grace,
>>>> everywhere we go. Amen.

**WORDS OF ASSURANCE (Revelation 7)**
> In God's love, we are held.
> In Christ's grace, we are forgiven.
> In the Spirit's power, we are strengthened.
> Give thanks for these marvelous gifts.

**PASSING THE PEACE OF CHRIST (Psalm 23, John 10, Festival of the Christian Home)**
> As we have been blessed with God's love and grace, may we bless one another by sharing signs of Christ's peace.

**RESPONSE TO THE WORD (Psalm 23)**
> The Lord is our shepherd.
> **We have all that we need.**
> God leads us in peace,
> **even through difficult journeys.**
> Surely God's goodness is enough,
> **all the days of our lives.**

# THANKSGIVING AND COMMUNION

### INVITATION TO THE OFFERING
As we prepare for this time of offering, may God open our hearts with love and touch our lives with generosity.

### OFFERING PRAYER (Psalm 23, John 10)
Generous God, we dedicate these gifts and offerings
into your service.
May our generosity flow abundantly
into a world in need
of your transforming love and grace.
In your loving name, we pray. Amen

# SENDING FORTH

### BENEDICTION (Psalm 23, John 10)
Blessed by God,
**may we bless the world in the week ahead.**
Loved by Christ,
**may we love others, in all we say and do.**
Empowered by the Spirit,
**may we follow faithfully where God leads.**

# Notes

# May 18, 2025

## Fifth Sunday of Easter

### B. J. Beu
*Copyright © B. J. Beu*

## COLOR

White

## SCRIPTURE READINGS

Acts 11:1-18; Psalm 148; Revelation 21:1-6;
John 13:31-35

## THEME IDEAS

God draws no distinction between peoples, for God
loves all equally. Through a vision, Peter is shown
that the Gentiles are to be included in the promises of
God. The psalmist calls creation to praise the creator of
heaven and earth. And Revelation promises that God
will wipe away every tear, for God has come to dwell
among us. Finally, John shares Jesus' commandment
to love one another, for his followers will be known by
their love.

# INVITATION AND GATHERING

## CENTERING WORDS (*John 13*)

They will know we are Christians by our love.

## CALL TO WORSHIP (*Acts 11, Revelation 21, John 13*)

The One who loves without distinction calls us here.
**They will know we are Christians by our love.**
The One who loves us completely welcomes us home.
**They will know we are Christians by our love.**
The One who loves us well rejoices in our presence.
**They will know we are Christians by our love.**

~or~

## CALL TO WORSHIP (*Psalm 148*)

From the highest heavens to the deepest seas,
**let all creation praise the Lord.**
From the rising sun to the waning moon,
**let all creatures praise the Lord.**
From the new heaven and new earth,
**let everything that draws breath praise the Lord.**
Come! Let us worship.

## OPENING PRAYER (*Revelation 21, John 13*)

Wipe away our tears, O God,
for we are weary of weeping
at the injustices of the world.
You love us like a mother
and protect us like a father.
You restore our lives
and claim us as your beloved children
in a world made new.
Dwell among us, we pray,
that we may love one another,
as you have loved us. Amen

# PROCLAMATION AND RESPONSE

*PRAYER OF YEARNING (Acts 11, John 13)*
Teach our hearts to love, O God,
as you would have us love.
Train our eyes to see, Holy One,
as you would have us see.
For we yearn to love without prejudice
and accept others without judgment.
Make your home among us,
for we long to be made one and whole. Amen.

*WORDS OF ASSURANCE (Acts 11, Psalm 148,*
*Revelation 21)*
The One who made heaven and earth is with us,
bringing love and life.
The Lord our God is among us now,
renewing us in faithful love.

*PASSING THE PEACE OF CHRIST (Acts 11)*
Look with the eyes of your heart enlightened, that you
may see one another as God sees you. Share the wonder of the vision before you, as you exchange signs of
Christ's peace.

*RESPONSE TO THE WORD (Acts 11, John 13)*
The Spirit falls upon God's people without partiality.
**They will know we are Christians by our love.**
The love of Christ is given to all without distinction.
**They will know we are Christians by our love.**
Let us fulfil Christ's Gospel by loving one another well.
**They will know we are Christians by our love.**

# THANKSGIVING AND COMMUNION

*INVITATION TO THE OFFERING (Revelation 21, John 13)*
    If we truly believed God dwells among us, would we
    live differently? Would we love differently? Would we
    give differently? Truly I tell you, God dwells among us
    even now. Let us share our faith and our love according-
    ly, as we collect this morning's offering.

*OFFERING PRAYER (Acts 11, John 13)*
    God of mystery, you promise us a life of blessedness,
        if only we would learn to love,
            as you have loved us.
    May the gifts we bring before you this day
        be a sign of our commitment
            to love one another well. Amen.

# SENDING FORTH

*BENEDICTION (John 13)*
    Christ has given us a new commandment.
    **We will love one another well.**
    God guides us to love the stranger.
    **We will love one another well.**
    The Spirit blesses with a new vision.
    **We will love one another well.**

# May 25, 2025

## Sixth Sunday of Easter

B. J. Beu
*Copyright © B. J. Beu*

## COLOR

White

## SCRIPTURE READINGS

Acts 16:9-15; Psalm 67; Revelation 21:1-10, 22–22:5; John 14:23-29

## THEME IDEAS

The Easter season is a time for sheer delight—a time to praise God with renewed faith and vision. The psalmist invites us to praise God for saving us, guiding us, and blessing us. The passage from Revelation provides a deeper sense of God's saving power, promising a new heaven and a new earth, where nations will walk in the light of the Lamb. Weeping will be no more, for God will wipe away every tear. The Gospel eases our sense of loss at Christ's departure, for God has sent us the Advocate, the Holy Spirit, to bring us peace, take away our fears, and lead us into truth. Take delight in God, for we are never alone on faith journeys.

MAY 25, 2025

# INVITATION AND GATHERING

*CALL TO WORSHIP (Psalm 67, John 14)*
Let the peoples praise you, O God.
**Let all the peoples praise you.**
Let all nations be glad and sing for joy.
**For you judge the peoples with justice and truth.**
Let the ends of the earth revere you, Holy One.
**For you bless your people with peace and hope.**

~or~

*CALL TO WORSHIP (Psalm 67)*
Sing and shout for joy.
**God's light shines upon us.**
Sing praises to God, sing praises.
**Let us worship the Lord.**

*OPENING PRAYER (Acts 16, John 14)*
Guiding Spirit, you come to us in visions and dreams,
showing us possibilities beyond our waking reality.
Open our hearts this day,
that we might understand Christ's teaching
and share his presence with others.
Guide our footsteps on our journeys,
that we might go where you send us
and share your message of love and peace
with the world. Amen.

# PROCLAMATION AND RESPONSE

*PRAYER OF YEARNING (John 14)*
God of love, help us keep your word
and love others as we ought.
For we long to let go of our suffering
and offer forgiveness to those
we have shut out of our hearts.

Send your Advocate to us once more,
   that we may feel Christ's promised peace
   and the release it brings.
May it be so, O God. May it be so.

## WORDS OF ASSURANCE (Revelation 21)

The One who is faithful will wipe away every tear
   and make all things new.
Walk in the light of the Lamb,
   in whom there is no darkness at all.
Receive grace from the one who brings us peace.

## PASSING THE PEACE OF CHRIST (

When Christ was about to depart this life, he promised
to send the Advocate, who would bring us peace, take
away our fears, and lead us into truth. Let us share signs
of this peace and this promise, as we pass the peace of
Christ.

## RESPONSE TO THE WORD (John 14)

Christ's words are true.
   **Teach us, Holy Spirit.**
Christ's words bring life.
   **Heal us, Holy Spirit.**
Christ is speaking still.
   **Lead us, Holy Spirit.**

~or~

## RESPONSE TO THE WORD (Easter)

Hear the good news of the one who conquered death.
Live the good news of the one who brings us life.
Share the good news of the one who leads us home.

# THANKSGIVING AND COMMUNION

*INVITATION TO THE OFFERING (Psalm 67, Revelation 21)*
> As we collect today's offering, may our gifts help wipe away one another's tears, even as we anticipate the time when God will dwell among us, wiping away every tear.

*OFFERING PRAYER (Psalm 67, Revelation 21)*
> Receive our praise, O God,
>> for the bounty of your love.
> You cause the earth to yield food
>> to satisfy the hungry.
> You send rain upon the earth
>> to give drink to the thirsty.
> You shine light into our darkness
>> to show us the way.
> Bless the gifts we bring before you this day,
>> that they may touch the world
>>> with your love. Amen.

# SENDING FORTH

*BENEDICTION (Revelation 21, John 14)*
> Embrace Christ's promised peace.
> Abide in God's promised home.
> Go in the power of the Holy Spirit.

~or~

*BENEDICTION (Revelation 21, John 14)*
> Hear Christ's words of peace:
>> "Peace I leave with you.
>> My peace I give to you."
> Rest in Christ's assurance of comfort:
>> "I do not give to you as the world gives."
>> Do not let your hearts be troubled,
>> and do not let them be afraid."
> Go in the peace and grace of Christ.

Notes

# June 1, 2025

## Ascension Sunday

### Mary Scifres
*Copyright © Mary Scifres*

## COLOR

White

## SCRIPTURE READINGS

Acts 1:1-11; Psalm 47; Ephesians 1:15-23; Luke 24:44-53

## ALTERNATE SCRIPTURE READINGS FOR SEVENTH SUNDAY OF EASTER

Acts 16:16-34; Psalm 97; Revelation 22:12-14, 16-17, 20-21; John 17:20-26

## THEME IDEAS

In our Ascension Day readings, God's glory takes flight, as Jesus ascends to the heavens. In our Seventh Sunday of Easter readings, God's glory settles on the disciples— first through Jesus' prayers, and then through the power of the Holy Spirit. Paul and Silas perform a dramatic healing and then personify deep faith as they sing and pray while imprisoned, bringing God's glory to their earthly work.

# INVITATION AND GATHERING

**CENTERING WORDS (Acts 1, Luke 24, Acts 16, Revelation 22, John 17)**
God's glory is seen, not just in the heavens, but in our everyday lives.

**CALL TO WORSHIP (Psalm 47, John 17)**
Clap your hands. Sing for joy!
**God's glory is all around.**
Rejoice and praise. Worship and pray.
**God's glory is in each of us.**

**OPENING PRAYER (Luke 24, John 17)**
God of grace and glory, shine through our worship,
that we may know your presence.
Shine through our lives,
that we may bring your presence to others.
Shine through our world,
that all may come to know you, love you,
and glorify your name. Amen.

# PROCLAMATION AND RESPONSE

**PRAYER OF YEARNING (Acts 16, Ephesians 1, John 17)**
From the demons that haunt our lives,
deliver us.
From the self-judgment and shame
that dim the light within us,
save us.
From the hurts and sorrows that harm us,
heal us.
Cover us with your comfort, grace, and love,
that we may shine with your glory and grace.
Amen.

**WORDS OF ASSURANCE (*Revelation 22*)**
Let the thirsty come.
For in Christ's grace, we receive the water of life.
In God's mercy, we receive forgiveness and love.

**RESPONSE TO THE WORD (*John 17*)**
Where do you see God's glory in the world?
Where does glory shine in your life?
How might you commit to shine more brightly
with God's glorious grace and love?

# THANKSGIVING AND COMMUNION

**INVITATION TO THE OFFERING (*Revelation 22*)**
Come! Let those who hear respond. Let those who respond offer the water of God's grace and love to a thirsty world.

**OFFERING PRAYER (*John 17, Revelation 22*)**
Glorious God, as we dedicate these gifts to you,
may we shine with your glory and grace.
Shine through these gifts and through our very lives,
that others may experience the beauty of your love
and the power of your presence. Amen.

# SENDING FORTH

**BENEDICTION (*John 17*)**
In the glory of God, go forth to shine with love.
Go forth to shine with peace.
Go forth to shine with hope for the world. Amen.

# Notes

# June 8, 2025

## Pentecost Sunday

### B. J. Beu
*Copyright © B. J. Beu*

## COLOR

Red

## SCRIPTURE READINGS

Acts 2:1-21; Psalm 104:24-34, 35b; Romans 8:14-17;
John 14:8-17, (25-27)

## THEME IDEAS

As Jesus' disciples huddled together in fear, the Holy
Spirit entered their dwelling in rushing wind and
tongues of fire. In that moment, the Church was born.
Without Pentecost, the disciples would not have had
the courage to go forth and spread the gospel. Because
of Pentecost, the Spirit, that was promised through the
prophet Joel, is active in our world today: granting
visions and dreams to old and young alike. The power of God to create and renew life is the power of the
Holy Spirit. We see this power in the psalmist's hymn
of praise. We behold this power in Paul's discussion of
adoption in Christ through the Spirit. And we receive
this power in Jesus, as he comforts his disciples before
his death.

# INVITATION AND GATHERING

### CENTERING WORDS (Acts 2)

Come and see the power of the Holy Spirit. Come and celebrate the birth of the church.

### CALL TO WORSHIP (Psalm 104)

O Lord, your works are wonderful!
**The earth is full of your handiwork.**
When you open your hand,
**we are filled with good things.**
When you take away our breath,
**we return to dust.**
Put your Spirit within us, O God,
**and renew us as your people.**

~or~

### CALL TO WORSHIP (Acts 2, John 14)

In rushing wind and cleansing fire . . .
**God's Spirit lead us here.**
In courage found and faith renewed . . .
**God's Spirit fills our hearts with longing.**
In visions seen and dreams made real . . .
**God's Spirit takes away our fear.**
In rushing wind and cleansing fire . . .
**God's Spirit sends us to share Christ's love.**

### OPENING PRAYER (Acts 2)

God of wind and flame, pour out your Holy Spirit
on a world in need of Pentecost fire.
Fill your people with courage and power,
and set our hearts ablaze,
that our young may have visions,
and our elders may dream dreams.
Ignite a passion within us to spread the good news
of your glorious salvation,
through Jesus Christ, our Lord. Amen.

# PROCLAMATION AND RESPONSE

*PRAYER OF YEARING (John 14)*
Eternal God, live in us on this day of Pentecost,
    as you live in your Son.
Draw us into communion with you
    and with one another,
        that we might glorify your name
            and reveal your majesty to the world.
Help us courageously keep your commandments,
    and boldly proclaim your mighty works,
        through the power of your Holy Spirit. Amen.

*WORDS OF ASSURANCE (Acts 2, Romans 8)*
The Spirit helps us in our weakness
    and removes our shame.
Rejoice, for God's steadfast love endures forever.
The Great Spirit leads us into life.

*PASSING THE PEACE OF CHRIST (John 14)*
God sent the Advocate to heal our divisions and to show
us the Way. Let us claim these blessings by sharing signs
of Christ's peace with one another.

*RESPONSE TO THE WORD (Acts 2, Romans 8)*
Can you feel it? God's Spirit draws us here.
    **Christ's Spirit washes over us.**
Will you embrace the Spirit's gifts?
    **God's Spirit ignites our dreams.**
The Spirit of Pentecost leads us once more.
    **Thanks be to God!**

# THANKSGIVING AND COMMUNION

### INVITATION TO THE OFFERING (Psalm 104)
When the Spirit breathes upon us, we are filled with good things. When this breath is taken away, we return to the dust of the earth. In the time we have, let us give thanks and share our blessing with the world.

### OFFERING PRAYER (Acts 2, Romans 8)
God of wind and flame, your Pentecost fire
    continues to touch us and bless our world today.
May our offering bring the warmth of your love,
    and the glory of your holy flame,
      to those who are shaken
        by the buffeting winds all around us. Amen.

# SENDING FORTH

### BENEDICTION (Acts 2, Romans 8)
Go, blessed by the power of God's Holy Spirit.
Go, warmed by God's sacred fire in your hearts.
Go, inspired by the glory of our Advocate.

Notes

141

# June 15, 2025

## Trinity Sunday
## Father's Day

### Leigh Ann Shaw

## COLOR

White

## SCRIPTURE READINGS

Proverbs 8:1-4, 22-31; Psalm 8; Romans 5:1-5;
John 16:12-15

## THEME IDEAS

Wisdom, the nature of God, and our connection with
God all peek out of today's scriptures. Psalm 8 gives
glory to the Sovereign Lord, recognizing elements of
creation as God's manifest work. The psalmist lauds the
God who creates and insists we claim our own role of
creation within God's order. Psalm 8 also names wisdom in the feminine. John 16 reflects Jesus' connection
within the Trinity, connecting him to the Spirit and the
Father. Romans offers a cornerstone of faith, reflecting
the Trinity and the relationship between Jesus, God, and
the Holy Spirit. The foundations of the Christian faith
loom large with these texts.

# INVITATION AND GATHERING

**CENTERING WORDS (Proverbs 8)**
Wisdom calls across the ages. Our ancestors in faith
heard and responded. By hearing and responding to the
Wisdom of the Ages, we meet God as Father, Son and
Spirit in worship this day.

**CALL TO WORSHIP (Psalm 8)**
Majestic God, your name rests upon our lips
    and opens our hearts to the blessings of life.
How is it that you care for each of us by name?
How is it that you come to one and all in worship?
How is it that in all your grandeur, we are not lost?
We worship you in thanksgiving and praise,
    rejoicing in your tender, abiding presence. Amen.

**OPENING PRAYER (Proverbs 8, Psalm 8, John 16)**
Holy Wisdom, Spirit of truth,
    your glory is written across the starry heavens;
    your wonder is etched in the earth and seas.
Who are we that you care for us so deeply?
Why do you love us so completely?
Raise your clarion call once more.
Speak to us this day,
    that our lives may be steeped in your wisdom,
        and our path may be marked with delight
            in your goodness. Amen.
*(B. J. Beu)*
*Copyright © B. J. Beu*

# PROCLAMATION AND RESPONSE

*PRAYER OF CONFESSION (Romans 5)*
Lord, we are often slow to trust your grace.
Distracted by the sufferings of daily living,
    we are compelled by the whims of grievance.
Thinking our strength is sufficient for any task or trial,
    we are brought to our knees.
When we think we can do everything ourselves,
    forgive us.
When we ignore your nudges toward spiritual growth,
    correct us.
Pour your Spirit within us again,
    that we might feel your love
        and remember who and whose we are. Amen.

*WORDS OF ASSURANCE (Romans 5)*
Friends and family of Christ, the Holy Spirit remains
    our counselor, our advocate, and our comforter.
Jesus Christ has restored all life to God.
In our faith, we are justified and made whole.

*PASSING OF THE PEACE (Romans 5)*
As we have been restored through faith and made
whole by the grace of God, let us offer signs of peace to
our family of faith.

*RESPONSE TO THE WORD (Proverbs 8)*
God's Word has been lifted.
God's Wisdom has been shared.
We are the people of God—
    people who have received God's Word
    and Wisdom. Amen.

# THANKSGIVING AND COMMUNION

*OFFERING PRAYER (Proverbs 8, Psalm 8)*
Lord of all creation, we celebrate the beauty
of your blessings each day.
With gratitude, we offer you these humble gifts.
Pour your spirit upon our tokens
and magnify them for your purposes,
that the world may come to know
the triune God. Amen.

# SENDING FORTH

*BENEDICTION (Romans 5)*
God's wisdom, beauty, and compassion bridge the ages
and meet us right where we are.
We have obtained an inheritance that is eternal.
Our hope is never in vain.
Let us hold fast as people justified by faith.
Let the love of God stir you and move you.
Let the Wisdom of the Ages shine through you,
as a beacon of God's love. Amen.

# ADDITIONAL RESOURCES

*AFFIRMATION OF FAITH*
I believe in God, Creator of all things seen and unseen,
rock, river, tree, animal, and force,
who made me and set me on my path in this world.

I believe in Jesus, beloved Son of the Creator,
who took on human form, was born of a woman,
through the power of the Holy Spirit,

and was raised within a family and community.
This man, Jesus of Nazareth, the Christ,
    made himself vulnerable to the world,
    endured the lies and violations of humanity,
    and withdrew only to pray and teach us
    the way of grace.
He walked a servant's path,
    through violence and death on the cross,
    rose from the dead, defeated the tomb
    and restored creation forever.

I believe in the Holy Spirit, my advocate
    and the mystery of Creation.
I believe this Spirit settled in my soul
    before I even drew breath,
    bringing me into communion with all people,
    past, present and future.
This Spirit calls me to be a pilgrim of a sacred way,
    to meet people where they are,
    and to show compassion and care.

I believe in the Kin-dom of all Creation,
    a family under the heavens,
    where no one is excluded, and all belong.
I believe I am called and claimed
    to be the hands and feet of the Kin-dom,
    to embrace life, share joy and love,
    and extend mercy to all. Amen.

Notes

# June 22, 2025

## Second Sunday after Pentecost
## Proper 7

### Mary Scifres

## COLOR

Green

## SCRIPTURE READINGS

1 Kings 19:1-4, (5-7), 8-15a; Psalm 42; Galatians 3:23-29; Luke 8:26-39

## THEME IDEAS

When fear runs the show, God calls us from the shadows, offers a healing touch, and invites us to move forward in the light of faith and hope. Even great prophets like Elijah knew the fear and despair that gripped the man possessed by demons. We long for God, yet fear tries to separate us from God. When fear tries to run the show, may hope and faith win the day.

# INVITATION AND GATHERING

**CENTERING WORDS** *(1 Kings 19, Psalm 42, Luke 8)*
When fear and despair try to run the show, hope and
faith bring us back to God, whose love is stronger still.

**CALL TO WORSHIP** *(Psalm 42, Luke 8)*
Come into the light of God's love.
**Fear cannot separate us from its blessing.**
Come to the house of healing and hope.
**God's love makes us whole.**

**OPENING PRAYER** *(1 Kings 19, Luke 8)*
God of power and might, bring your awesome presence
into our worship and our world.
Open us to your wholeness and healing
and embolden us to answer your call,
that we might face unafraid
the demons of this world. Amen.

# PROCLAMATION AND RESPONSE

**PRAYER OF YEARNING** *(1 Kings 19, Luke 8)*
Loving God, we yearn to be close to you
and to dwell in your ever-present love.
Be with us when our yearning seems unsatisfied.
Great Healer, bring us the help we most need.
Wipe away our fears.
Comfort us in our regrets.
Forgive our mistakes.
Strengthen us with healing and hope.
Draw us so close to you,
that we may never question your presence
or have reason to be afraid. Amen.

**WORDS OF ASSURANCE (Galatians 3, Luke 8)**
Before faith, we were locked away in our fear.
But faith is ours through the grace of Christ.
In this grace, we are no longer chained;
we are no longer bound by demons, regrets, or sin.
We are freed with love, freed to love,
and freed to be loved.

**RESPONSE TO THE WORD (1 Kings 19, Psalm 42, Luke 8)**
*(Offer these questions slowly with time for silent reflection. Or invite people to jot down a few notes to themselves as they reflect on these questions. You might pause after the last question before offering the last three sentences of blessing.)*

What demons are haunting you?
What regrets are holding you back?
What fears are causing you to hide?
What sorrows are in need of comfort?
What ills are in need of healing?

Put your trust in God,
for God's healing is real.
Commit your life to God,
for God's strength is sure.
Place your hope in God,
for God's love is with us now and forevermore.

# THANKSGIVING AND COMMUNION

**INVITATION TO THE OFFERING (Luke 8)**
As we have been healed and strengthened by Christ, so now Christ invites us to offer healing and strength to the world through our gifts and our lives.

*OFFERING PRAYER (Psalm 42, Luke 8)*
>Healer of life's ills, bring healing and strength
>>through the gifts we bring before you now.
>Bring hope, faith, and love,
>>that our church may be an instrument of healing
>>>and a vessel of hope for a hurting world. Amen.

# SENDING FORTH

*BENEDICTION (Luke 8)*
>Don't just hang out with Christ this week;
>>bring Christ to everyone you meet.
>This is what Jesus invites us to do.
>This is the faithful response to the many ways
>>Christ has healed and saved us.
>Amen.

Notes

# June 29, 2025

## Third Sunday after Pentecost
## Proper 8

### Kirsten Linford

## COLOR

Green

## SCRIPTURE READINGS

2 Kings 2:1-2, 6-14; Psalm 77:1-2, 11-20;
Galatians 5:1, 13-25; Luke 9:51-62

## THEME IDEAS

Woven through these scriptures are themes of leave-taking, faithful accompaniment, passing the mantle of leadership, commitment, and covenant. As Elijah and Jesus prepare to depart from their lives, they must prepare others to continue on without them. Each leader calls on their followers to keep their eyes open and watch all the way to the end, lest they miss the calling that is to be placed upon them. Galatians reminds us that God's call, and our covenant with God and one another, are meant to be defined by service, rather than submission. The psalm feels like a prayer we might hear from Elisha or any of the disciples, as they seek to respond faithfully.

# INVITATION AND GATHERING

## CENTERING WORDS (2 Kings)

When Elijah was about to taken from him, Elisha asked
for a double portion of his spirit. May we too recognize
our need and have the courage to ask for what we need
to do our ministries.

## CALL TO WORSHIP (Psalm 77)

We will call to mind the works of the Lord,
  **and remember God's wonders of old.**
In times of trouble, we cry out to God,
  **longing for our souls to be comforted.**
When our spirits are weary,
  **we reach for God's arms.**
Even when we don't feel courageous,
  **we need to receive God's peace.**
Keeping God's deeds in mind,
  **we carry them in our hearts.**
For God's ways are holy,
  **and God's grace is great.**

## OPENING PRAYER (Psalm 77)

Holy One, the waters tremble
  and the skies open.
Your voice rumbles with thunder,
  flashes with lightning,
    and crashes with waves
      as the earth shakes.
And yet, there is peace in your voice.
You trouble the waters of our spirits,
  even as you soothe the struggles of our souls.
Your footprints guide our way—
  unseen by human eyes,
    but always visible to our hearts. Amen.

# PROCLAMATION AND RESPONSE

**PRAYER OF YEARNING** *(2 Kings 2, Luke 9)*

God of our lives, we set our sights on you.
For you know where you are going,
> and long for us to follow.
It is not easy to keep our eyes upon you, God,
> and watch until the end.
We often look away and maintain our denial,
> just a little longer.
But denial never serves us.
It is truth we need;
> courage and strength we desire.
Enough to face this day and the next . . .
> enough to stay with you as you stay with us . . .
> enough to inherit your Spirit,
>> the whole of it and a double share as well . . .
> enough to follow you to the end . . .
> and beyond. Amen.

**WORDS OF ASSURANCE** *(2 Kings 2, Luke 9)*

Jesus says, "Follow me."
When we stay with him,
> he always stays with us.
God places the Spirit upon us and within us,
> trusting us to watch and follow.
The Holy One calls us to reach out our hands
> and receive God's mantle of leadership.
Believing that we can, we will.

**PASSING THE PEACE OF CHRIST** *(2 Kings 2)*

Let us share the words of our ancestor, Elisha: "As the
Lord lives, and as you yourself life, I will not leave you."
Let us walk together in peace.

*PRAYER OF PREPARATION (Psalm 19)*
    May the words of my mouth . . .
        **and the meditations of our hearts**
            **be acceptable in your sight, O Lord,**
                **our strength and our redeemer. Amen.**

*RESPONSE TO THE WORD (Galatians 5)*
    For freedom, Christ has set us free.
    Let us stand firm, therefore—
        not in submission, but in service;
        not in coercion, but in calling;
        not compelled, but with commitment, covenant,
           and choice.
    Let us stand in communion
        and carry Christ's call for any and for all. Amen.

# THANKSGIVING AND COMMUNION

*INVITATION TO THE OFFERING (2 Kings 2)*
    God has given us a calling and equipped us with an
    abundant share of God's own Spirit—gifts to use and
    to share.

*OFFERING PRAYER (2 Kings 2, Galatians 5)*
    Gracious God, you have put your Spirit within us
        and laid your mantle upon us.
    These are gifts we could never earn
        and can never repay.
    Yet we are filled with your love, joy, patience,
        peace, generosity, faithfulness, gentleness,
           and self-control.
    And so we offer them all to you,
        grateful to pass them on to your people
           and to your world. Amen.

# SENDING FORTH

**BENEDICTION (2 *Kings* 2)**
People of God, the mantle of God's love and mercy
  is upon you.
Carry it with you, as you go and serve. Amen.

Notes

# July 6, 2025

## Fourth Sunday after Pentecost
## Proper 9

### Amy B. Hunter

## COLOR

Green

## SCRIPTURE READINGS

2 Kings 5:1-14; Galatians 6:(1-6) 7-16; Luke 10:1-11, 16-20

## THEME IDEAS

*The Kingdom of God has come near!* Too often, we miss being part of this inbreaking presence. Instead we distract ourselves with concerns for reputation, power, rules, and success. These lections remind us that this struggle is as old as humanity itself. Our call, then and now, is to trust God—the One who speaks through the powerless, disregards our rules, and rescues us by the Cross. God's inbreaking kingdom moves us to love one another, share each other's struggles, and receive others with peace.

# INVITATION AND GATHERING

**CENTERING WORDS (*Luke 10*)**
The Kingdom of God has come near. Draw near to God.

**CALL TO WORSHIP (*2 Kings 5, Galatians 6, Luke 10*)**
All are welcome here. Whether you are heavy-hearted,
wondering if there is power to make you well,
or feel weighed down by many demands,
    **The kingdom of God has come near.**
Whether you are burdened by rules others have imposed
or you are a keeper and maker of rules,
    **The kingdom of God has come near.**
Whether you feel at home in this place
or you long to be accepted,
    **The kingdom of God has come near.**
Come and worship God, the One who writes
our names in the book of life and dares us
to be become new creations in Jesus.
    **The kingdom of God has come near.**

**OPENING PRAYER (*Galatians 6, Luke 10*)**
Challenging God, you send us out
    like lambs among wolves,
        then ask us to be peaceful and gentle.
Help us hear and obey your call to follow Jesus,
    even if we must surrender our reputations
        and rules we hold dear.
May we learn and live the path of the cross,
    restoring one another
        and bearing one another's burdens,
            as we discover your gift
                of becoming new creations in Christ.
Amen.

# PROCLAMATION AND RESPONSE

**PRAYER OF YEARNING *(Psalm 30, Luke 10)***
Peaceful and merciful God, you promise
    that your Kingdom is within our reach.
Yet we are often distracted by disagreements,
    demands, requirements, and rejections.
    **Have mercy O Lord; be our helper.**
As we seek to follow Jesus,
    our rules and offences can separate us.
Help us to refrain from deepening our divisions,
    and empower us to restore one another,
        fulfilling Christ's command to love.
    **Have mercy O Lord; be our helper.**
You promise us victory over all
    that threatens to separate us from your presence.
Help us forsake earthly power and victory,
    as we strive for the love your kingdom brings.
    **Have mercy O Lord; be our helper.**
We ask for your grace to become more like Jesus,
    letting go of fleeting rewards
        of earthly status and recognition.
Help us seek instead the eternal reward
    of resting in your loving arms.
    **Have mercy O Lord; be our helper. Amen.**

**WORDS OF ASSURANCE *(Psalm 30)***
People of God, God hears us and has mercy.
God turns our wailing into dancing
    and our deepest regrets in our greatest joys.
    **O Lord, our hearts sing to you.**
    **We give you thanks forever.**

**PASSING THE PEACE OF CHRIST (Luke 10)**
Jesus entreats us to enter the spaces of our lives, offering
peace to those we meet. Let us greet one another with
signs of this welcoming peace.

**INTRODUCTION TO THE WORD (Luke 10)**
Let us listen to God's Word today,
knowing that the kingdom of God is near.

**RESPONSE TO THE WORD (Luke 10)**
We have heard of God's inbreaking kingdom.
**Let us welcome God's Word,
rejoicing that our names are written in heaven.**

# THANKSGIVING AND COMMUNION

**INVITATION TO THE OFFERING (Galatians 6)**
Beloved people of God, let us give to the work of God's
kingdom today. May we take this opportunity to work
for the common good, and especially for the family of
faith.

**OFFERING PRAYER (Galatians 6, Luke 10)**
Generous God, you share your kingdom
with all humanity,
drawing closer to us than our very breath.
May our offering this day support your holy work,
and may all come to know
that your kingdom has truly come near. Amen.

# SENDING FORTH

**BENEDICTION** *(Galatians 6, Luke 10)*
    May the Lord of the harvest,
        who sent the disciples out as ambassadors for Christ,
        send you out to proclaim that the kingdom of God
        has drawn near.
    May Jesus Christ,
        who gave authority to heal and to resist evil,
        bless you with the knowledge that your names
        are written in heaven.
    May the Holy Spirit,
        who gives you the power to persevere,
        send you to care for one another,
        sowing seeds of the Spirit
        and reaping the harvest of eternal life.

# Notes

# July 13, 2025

## Fifth Sunday after Pentecost
## Proper 10

### Mary Scifres
*Copyright © Mary Scifres*

## COLOR

Green

## SCRIPTURE READINGS

Amos 7:7-17; Psalm 82; Colossians 1:1-14; Luke 10:25-37

## THEME IDEAS

Love of God and neighbor are the greatest commandments and lie at the center of today's scriptures. Amos'
prophetic word of judgment is a response to the failure
to love one's neighbor. The prophet brings God's warn-
ing against wealth inequity, leaving the poor without
compassion, and failing to care for the community of
faith. The Colossian church is lauded for the precise op-
posite—for their love of all God's people, for bearing
fruit, and for growing spiritually together. Jesus' parable
of the Good Samaritan illustrates vividly that we are to
care for our neighbors with compassion and generosity.

# INVITATION AND GATHERING

**CENTERING WORDS** *(Amos 7, Psalm 82, Colossians 1, Luke 10)*

If we are all people of God, who is our neighbor? The sinner, the saint, the outcast, the beloved, the oppressed, the powerful, the poor, and the wealthy. We all need God's love; we all need to love one another.

**CALL TO WORSHIP** *(Colossians 1, Luke 10)*

Beloved people of God, welcome to worship.
**We come to worship and to praise.**
With love for one another, we gather as neighbors.
**With love for God, we gather as God's**
**community of love.**

**OPENING PRAYER** *(Colossians 1, Luke 10)*

Loving God, thank you for being present in our lives
and in this time of worship.
Speak love to our hearts and wisdom to our minds,
that we might grow in your knowledge of love
and that our lives might bear the fruit
of your knowledge and grace. Amen.

**PRAYER OF YEARNING** *(Psalm 82, Luke 10)*

Merciful God, help us remember to love and care
for our neighbors.
When we would rather walk around people in need
and avoid situations that trouble us,
soften our hearts.
Give us the courage to care for our neighbors
and to love others as graciously
as you love us.
In your grace and love, we pray. Amen.

## WORDS OF ASSURANCE

In grace, we are strengthened.
In love, our hearts are freed.
In God, grace and love are ours.

## PASSING THE PEACE OF CHRIST (Colossians 1, Luke 10)

As neighbors and friends, let's share our love in the Spirit with signs of peace.

## INTRODUCTION TO THE WORD (Colossians 1)

May the message of God's Spirit fill us with knowledge, wisdom, and spiritual understanding.

## RESPONSE TO THE WORD (Luke 10)

*(A time of silence may follow each sentence, or you may invite people to lift names aloud or in their online chat.)*

Take a moment to give thanks for neighbors
    in this place.
Take a moment to give thanks for neighbors
    in our community.
Take a moment to give thanks for neighbors
    in our world.
Take a moment to give thanks for those who have cared
    for us when we have been neighbors in need.
Thanks be to God for these amazing gifts.

# THANKSGIVING AND COMMUNION

## INVITATION TO THE OFFERING (Colossians 1, Luke 10)

May the gifts we bring bear the fruit of God's love to our neighbors around the world.

**OFFERING PRAYER (Amos 7, Psalm 82, Luke 10)**
Gracious God, bless these gifts.
May they bring your love, justice, and compassion
to where they are most needed in our world.
Help us be good neighbors to everyone we meet.
With gratitude and love, we pray. Amen.

# SENDING FORTH

**BENEDICTION (Psalm 82, Luke 10)**
Bring loving compassion to your homes.
Bring loving compassion to your neighborhoods.
Bring loving compassion to everyone you meet.
Go as God's blessings to the world.

Notes

# July 20, 2025

## Sixth Sunday after Pentecost
## Proper 11

### B. J. Beu
*Copyright © B. J. Beu*

## COLOR

Green

## SCRIPTURE READINGS

Amos 8:1-12; Psalm 52; Colossians 1:15-28;
Luke 10:38-42

## THEME IDEAS

Where judgment and lamentation pervade today's Hebrew Scripture readings, hope and assurance dominate today's New Testament texts. Due to people's evil deeds, Amos proclaims a famine of the word—they will seek it but find it not. And while the psalmist warns of the impending destruction of those who do evil, there is good news for the righteous—they will be like green olive trees in the house of God. In Colossians, Paul proclaims that we are reconciled to God in Christ. In Luke's Gospel, Jesus reproofs Martha for being distracted by her duties, even as he lifts Mary for choosing to sit in his presence.

# INVITATION AND GATHERING

### CENTERING WORDS (Psalm 52)
The righteous are like green olive trees in the house of the Lord. They will dwell in God's steadfast love forever and ever.

### CALL TO WORSHIP (Psalm 52)
We come into God's presence,
**like green olive trees in the house of God.**
We drink deep from the waters of life,
**like young saplings in the courtyard of the Lord.**
We ripen in the light of God,
**like the fruit of God's vineyard.**
Come! Let us worship.

### OPENING PRAYER (Amos 8, Psalm 52, Luke 10)
Loving God, your presence in our lives
is like a green olive tree—
a joy to the heart
and a blessing to the spirit.
Your movement in our midst
is like a basket of summer fruit—
a delight to the eye
and a pleasure to the tongue.
Speak to us your words of life,
that we may sit at your feet
and know that we are yours. Amen.

# PROCLAMATION AND RESPONSE

### PRAYER OF YEARNING (Amos 8, Psalm 52, Colossians 1)
When the winds of life buffet us, O God,
we need your hand to hold us
and your love to make us whole.

Speak words of peace to our aching hearts,
> that we might find the courage
>> to embrace the fullness of life
>>> you place before us.
Correct our sight when our vision fades,
> and lead in right paths when we lose our way.
Amen.

## WORDS OF ASSURANCE (Colossians 1)

There is no condemnation in Christ.
In his mercy, we are united and reconciled with God.
Rejoice that we find abundant life in his name.

## PASSING THE PEACE OF CHRIST (Colossians 1)

In Christ, we find peace, a gift beyond price, as we are reconciled to God. Let us share this precious gift with one another in joy and thanksgiving, as we pass the peace of Christ with one another.

## RESPONSE TO THE WORD (Amos 8)

Our hearts are famished.
**We are hungry for God's Word.**
May the words we have heard take root in our hearts.
**May the wisdom they teach take root in our lives.**
Our hearts are famished.
**We are hungry for God's Word.**

# THANKSGIVING AND COMMUNION

## OFFERING PRAYER (Amos 8)

Loving God, like baskets of summer fruit,
> you fill our lives to overflowing.
May the offering we return to you this day
> reflect our gratitude for your many blessings.

May they show our commitment
    to love our neighbors as we love ourselves.
Through your goodness and the sharing of these gifts,
    may the world come to know
        the richness of your love. Amen.

# SENDING FORTH

**BENEDICTION (Psalm 52)**
Though we may leave God's house,
    **we do not leave God's presence.**
Like green olive trees in the house of God,
    **we will plant our roots in the soil of holy love.**
Heeding the joy of God's call in our lives,
    **we go to share God's love for all.**

**Notes**

# July 27, 2025

## Seventh Sunday after Pentecost
## Proper 12

### Mary Scifres
*Copyright © Mary Scifres*

## COLOR

Green

## SCRIPTURE READINGS

Hosea 1:2-10; Psalm 85; Colossians 2:6-15, (16-19); Luke 11:1-13

## THEME IDEAS

Today's scriptures invite us to draw closer to God in a variety of ways. The Israelites must repent and return to God, if they are to embrace their blessings as "children of the living God." These texts remind us of the danger of wandering away and abandoning the God who both creates and saves us. The letter to the Colossians advises us to remain close to God, by being rooted in Christ and growing in faith with overflowing gratitude. And Jesus guides his disciples, then and now, to communicate so intimately and trustingly with God, that when they ask, God will answer.

# INVITATION AND GATHERING

**CENTERING WORDS** *(Colossians 2, Luke 11)*
In our asking and in our seeking, let us find strength
and growth from the root of our lives, Christ Jesus.

**CALL TO WORSHIP** *(Luke 11)*
Before we even knock,
**Christ opens the doors and invites us in.**
Before we even ask,
**God knows our every need.**
Come to seek; come to pray; come to worship,
**for the Spirit has called us here.**

**OPENING PRAYER** *(Luke 11)*
Sustaining God, grant us our basic needs.
Where there is hunger,
give us bread.
Where there is homelessness,
give us shelter.
Where there is loneliness,
give us friendship.
Where we have wronged another,
guide us into reconciliation.
And where we have been wronged,
lead us on the journey of forgiveness.
Save in times of trial,
and lead us in the Way of life. Amen.

~or~

**OPENING PRAYER** *(Luke 11)*
Christ Jesus, we come to your house this day,
knocking and asking that the door may be opened.
We come seeking your face
and yearning for your presence in our lives.

Open the door of our hearts,
    as you have opened the doors of your church.
Lift our faces,
    that we may see your face shining upon us.
Answer our yearning,
    that our restive hearts may find their rest in you.
Amen.

# PROCLAMATION AND RESPONSE

## CALL TO PRAYER (Luke 11)
Ask, for God is listening
Seek, for God will find you.
Pray, for God is with us.

## PRAYER OF YEARNING (Colossians 2, Luke 11)
Grow in our lives, Christ Jesus.
Make our hearts larger
    with each gift of your grace.
Make our spirits stronger
    with each moment of your mercy.
As you fill our lives with your presence,
    fill our hearts with your love,
        that we might grow into your likeness.
As we grow in your love,
    may we give our love and grace as freely
        as you have generously given your love to us.
Amen.

## WORDS OF ASSURANCE (Colossians 2)
In the grace of Christ, we are connected to God's love,
    both now and forevermore. Amen.

## PASSING THE PEACE OF CHRIST (Psalm 85)
In faithful love, let us share signs of peace and kindness
with one another.

*INTRODUCTION TO THE WORD (Colossians 2)*
>    May we receive nourishment in God's Word,
>    and may it establish our faith and grow Christ's love
>    in our lives.

*RESPONSE TO THE WORD (Luke 11)*
>    As we ask,
>    **God hears our need.**
>    As we seek,
>    **God holds us.**
>    As we knock,
>    **God answers with grace and love.**

# THANKSGIVING AND COMMUNION

*INVITATION TO THE OFFERING (Colossians 2)*
>    We have been gifted and loved generously by God. In
>    turn, may we share our gifts and love through God's
>    work in the world.

*OFFERING PRAYER (Hosea 1, Colossians 2)*
>    God of love and justice,
>        our hearts are filled with gratitude
>            for all that you have given us.
>    As we share these gifts with you,
>        bless them and our ministries,
>            that they may bring love and justice
>                to your world. Amen.

# SENDING FORTH

*BENEDICTION (Colossians 2)*
>    Rooted in Christ,
>    grow in faith and love.
>    Growing in love and faith,
>    give these blessings to the world.

# August 3, 2025

## Eighth Sunday after Pentecost
## Proper 13

### Michelle L. Torigian

## COLOR

Green

## SCRIPTURE READINGS

Hosea 11:1-11; Psalm 107:1-9, 43; Colossians 3:1-11;
Luke 12:13-21

## THEME IDEAS

Colossians 3 says, "Set your minds on things that are
above, not on the things that are on earth" (v. 2, NRSVue).
Today's texts center our minds and souls on the realm
of God. Often, we are drawn by unhealthy paths on this
earth—from greed to behaviors that hurt our neighbors.
As we clothe ourselves with the gifts of God and the
knowledge that we are made in God's image, let us use
our resources to build the realm of God here on earth.
Today, we embody a spirit of renewal, embrace the love
of God, and work to share this love with our siblings,
with whom we share an eternal connection.

# INVITATION AND GATHERING

*CENTERING PRAYER (Colossians 3)*
May the kindling of God warm our souls. May the winds of the Spirit nudge us onward. May the love of Christ transform us anew.

~or~

*CENTERING PRAYER (Colossians 3)*
Breathe in holy love. Shine with holy light.

*CALL TO WORSHIP (Psalm 107)*
Give thanks to God,
**for God's steadfast love lasts forever.**
God accompanies us in our distress,
**as we cross the threshold to worship's blessings.**
Give thanks to our God,
**for God's steadfast love abides with us.**
Let us enter this space for worship,
**celebrating God's works for humankind.**

*OPENING PRAYER (Psalm 107, Colossians 3, Luke 12)*
Spirit of hope and renewal,
as the dawn nudges us awake,
summon us with your presence.
Wrap us with the cloak of your wisdom and grace.
As your light breaks the horizon this day,
help us see the love revealed in your realm.
Nourish us with your wisdom
and guide us with your hope,
for we hunger to know you better. Amen.

# PROCLAMATION AND RESPONSE

**PRAYER OF YEARNING** *(Hosea 11, Colossians 3, Luke 12)*
Loving God, Divine Guide,
>may we not turn away from you
>>as our desires take hold.

When we are drawn to the sparkle around us,
>draw us back to the holy glow of your realm.

When we focus on the divisions that divide us,
>lead us to share your steadfast love
>>with those we are separated from.

When we fixate on how to get ahead,
>move us to share your bounty with our neighbors.

Draw us back to you, Holy Beacon of Hope
>that we might all be made well. Amen.

**WORDS OF ASSURANCE** *(Psalm 107)*
The steadfast love of God radiates within our spirits,
>encouraging us to abandon unhealthy paths.

God's grace fills our hearts with hope,
>as we rejoice in God's redeeming presence.

**PASSING THE PEACE OF CHRIST** *(Hosea 11)*
Through bands of love, we are forever connected. May
we share the peace of Christ, the love of God, and the
comfort of the Holy Spirit, knowing that the cords of
human kindness bind us together throughout eternity.

**RESPONSE TO THE WORD** *(Colossians 3)*
May the Spirit of God clothe our minds with wisdom.
May the redemption we find in Christ
>clothe our hearts with hope.

May our Divine Designer clothe our souls
>with a refreshing sense of awe.

# THANKSGIVING AND COMMUNION

### INVITATION TO OFFERING (Luke 12)
The many gifts that we hold in our hands and souls have the power and potential to strengthen the lives of God's children everywhere. As we seek ways to celebrate our gifts, let us utilize our gifts, not only for ourselves, but to build the fullness of God's realm here on earth.

### OFFERING PRAYER (Colossians 3, Luke 12)
God of Goodness, thank you for your steadfast love
   and your wonderful works.
Today we stand in front of you with our riches in hand:
   our treasures, time, and talents.
May our giving reflect the faithfulness of our spirits.
And may our offering be clothed
   with your visions and dreams. Amen.

# SENDING FORTH

### BENEDICTION (Hosea 11, Psalm 107, Colossians 3)
May we secure the cords of kindness
   and the bands of love on the path forward.
May we clothe ourselves in cloaks of renewal,
   building the realm of God here on earth.
May we celebrate the steadfast love of God
   and embracing Christ's presence.
Surely God journeys with us forever. Amen!

# Notes

# August 10, 2025

## Ninth Sunday after Pentecost
## Proper 14

### Michael Beu

## COLOR

Green

## SCRIPTURE READINGS

Isaiah 1:1, 10-20; Psalm 50:1-8, 22-23;
Hebrews 11:1-3, 8-16; Luke 12:32-40

## THEME IDEAS

Isaiah, the psalmist, and Luke make clear that if our actions do not embody justice and righteous, even worshiping the "right way" is spiritually empty and is not pleasing to God. God will not listen to the prayers of those who trample the weak and whose hands are full of blood. The psalmist adds that our God is a devouring fire, and those who do not repent of their errant ways will be utterly swept away. Still, those who live according to God's precepts will know the glory of salvation in Christ. In Luke, Jesus tells us not to worry, for it is God's pleasure to give us the kingdom. Still, Jesus warns that we should store up treasures in heaven, not on earth—for where our treasure is, there our hearts will be also.

# INVITATION AND GATHERING

### CENTERING WORDS *(Luke 12)*

Do not be afraid little flock, it is God's good pleasure to give you the kingdom.

~or~

### CENTERING WORDS *(Luke 12:34 NRSV)*

"Where your treasure is, there your heart will be also" (Luke 12:34).

### CALL TO WORSHIP *(Psalm 50, Luke 12)*

From the rising to the setting sun,
**God summons us.**
In the perfect beauty all around us,
**God brightens our hearts.**
When we worship with acts of love and mercy,
**God is pleased to give us the kingdom.**
Come! Let justice and righteousness be our worship.

### OPENING PRAYER *(Isaiah 1, Luke 12)*

Mighty God, dress us for action,
for the world is in need of our care.
Turn us from our selfish ways
and help us share the fat of this good land.
For when we refuse and rebel,
we reap what we have sown.
Your care and compassion call to us.
Your mercy and grace reach out to us.
Heal us day,
and may it be your good pleasure
to give us the kingdom.

# PROCLAMATION AND RESPONSE

*PRAYER OF YEARNING (Isaiah 1, Luke 12)*
When our prayers and devotions
    are divorced from works of love and justice,
        we long to return to your ways.
Wash us with your grace and mercy
    and help us store up treasure in heaven
        where neither thief nor moth destroy.
Remove the evil we harbor in our hearts,
    and transform our selfish deeds
        into acts of righteousness.
In your holy name, we pray. Amen.

*WORDS OF ASSURANCE (Luke 12)*
Don't be afraid, little flock.
God delights in giving us the kingdom.

*PASSING THE PEACE OF CHRIST (Luke 12)*
It is God's good pleasure to give us the kingdom. Let us share this treasure with one another as we pass the peace of Christ.

*INTRODUCTION TO THE WORD (Isaiah 1, Psalm 50)*
Listen for the Word of God,
    for God is still speaking.

*RESPONSE TO THE WORD (Isaiah 1, Luke 12)*
Be ready.
    **God comes at unexpected times**
    **and in unexpected places.**
Prepare to work.
    **God requires our hands and feet,**
    **as well as our hearts and minds.**
Dress with love and compassion.
    **God asks us to keep our lamps lit**
    **and to be the light of the world.**

# THANKSGIVING AND COMMUNION

### INVITATION TO THE OFFERING (Luke 12)
Where our treasure is, there our hearts will be also. Let
us bring the treasure of our love.

### OFFERING PRAYER (Luke 12)
God of grace and God of glory,
>    transform these gifts
>>        into vessels of your love and mercy.
By the power of your Holy Spirit,
>    may our offering bring treasure from above.
May these gifts bring justice and righteousness
>    to your children everywhere. Amen.

# SENDING FORTH

### BENEDICTION (Luke 12)
People get ready.
**We are dressed for love.**
People get ready.
**We are dressed for service.**
People get ready.
**We are dressed to shine Christ's light.**

# Notes

# August 17, 2025

## Tenth Sunday after Pentecost
## Proper 15

### James Dollins

## COLOR

Green

## SCRIPTURE READINGS

Isaiah 5:1-7; Psalm 80:1-2, 8-19; Hebrews 11:29–12:2;
Luke 12:49-56

## THEME IDEAS

One of scripture's greatest assurances is that we are not
alone. When we look to God with faith, we join millen-
nia of those who believe in God's goodness, however
bleak circumstances may be. While today's readings al-
lude to oppression, exile, and tribulation, we hear, especially in Hebrews 11, a call to persevering faith. Thankfully, when we feel least powerful, God blesses us with
faith, which cannot be taken from us.

# INVITATION AND GATHERING

**CENTERING WORDS (Hebrews 11)**
When life startles and upsets, faith looks forward. When questions and doubts arise, faith knows that God will prevail. Remember who you are and what God's love can do.

**CALL TO WORSHIP (Psalm 80)**
Give ear, God of all people.
**Stir up your strength and deliver us!**
Once you rescued your children from bondage.
**Now, set your people free.**
Look down from heaven, God of hosts.
**Turn to us anew and see us in our need.**
Restore us, God of Creation.
**Let your face shine upon us.**
May our suffering cease.
**May all your children be saved.**

**OPENING PRAYER (Hebrews 11)**
Come, Holy Spirit.
Hear our prayers and songs of praise.
We join voices from ancient times,
    that placed their trust you
        in days of joy or pain.
Inspire us in this hour,
    that we may never surrender to despair.
Renew in us enduring faith,
    even as we join eternally in song. Amen.

# PROCLAMATION AND RESPONSE

***PRAYER OF CONFESSION or PRAYER OF YEARNING***
***(Hebrews 11)***
   We give thanks, Precious Lord,
     that your love casts out fear,
      that your life transcends death itself.
   You simply ask that we maintain a posture of faith,
     with eyes open to the future you will bring.
   Forgive us when we pre-judge where we will,
     or will not, see you.
   We decide too soon whom we will listen to
     and whom we will dismiss.
   Forgive us; awaken us; restore our faith in you,
     that we may find new faith in ourselves
      and in the neighbors we meet. Amen.

***WORDS OF ASSURANCE (Hebrews 11, Ephesians 2)***
   By faith, we have been saved through faith.
   This is not our own doing; it is the gift of God.
   In the name of Christ you are forgiven.
   **In the name of Christ you are forgiven.**
   **Thanks be to God. Amen.**

***RESPONSE TO THE WORD (Hebrews 11)***
   Even without understanding, amid confusion and trials,
   our ancestors in faith looked to God for strength.
   Let us follow in their ways:
   **The good works to which we are called**
   **are too essential to be neglected.**
   The world needs peace too badly
   for us to become mired in despair.
   **With our ancestors in faith before us,**
   **we will offer our hope, our dreams,**
   **and our trust that God's love lives even now.**

In faith, feed others in body and spirit,
as we stand together against injustice.
**We will participate in the life-saving work
of Christ, our Lord. Amen.**

*OFFERING PRAYER (Hebrews 11)*
Faith is the assurance of things hoped for,
the conviction of things not seen.
Yet how good it is to see living acts of faith
in Christ's church and its people.
Bless, O Lord, the offerings we give,
that others may know your love,
and come to trust your provision and peace.
Amen.

## SENDING FORTH

*BENEDICTION (Hebrews 11)*
Truly we are surrounded by a great cloud of witnesses.
Let us live and love, as these examples of faith
have shown us how. Amen.

# Notes

# August 24, 2025

## Eleventh Sunday after Pentecost
## Proper 16

### B. J. Beu
*Copyright © B. J. Beu*

## COLOR

Green

## SCRIPTURE READINGS

Jeremiah 1:4-10; Psalm 71:1-6; Hebrews 12:18-29;
Luke 13:10-17

## THEME IDEAS

The theme of rescue runs through today's scriptures.
Before Jeremiah was even born, God had consecrated
him to be a prophet—to rescue God's people from aimlessness and sin. The psalmist invites us to seek refuge
in the One who rescues us from earthly perils. Hebrews
proclaims that the whole created order will be shaken,
and that Christ has come to rescue us from all that does
not endure. In Luke, Jesus rescues a woman from an in-
firmity that has afflicted her for 18 years. In a world full
of peril, rebellion, and decay, God rescues us and offers
us a kingdom that cannot be shaken.

# INVITATION AND GATHERING

**CENTERING WORDS (Psalm 71)**
    The Lord is our fortress, a refuge in times of trouble.

**CALL TO WORSHIP (Jeremiah 1, Psalm 71, Luke 13)**
    The Lord is our rock and our refuge.
        **God is our fortress in times of trouble.**
    The Holy One saves us from the hand of the wicked.
        **God delivers us from our foes.**
    Christ heals us from our infirmities.
        **The Spirit frees us from the chains that bind us.**
    Rest in the Source of our refuge and our strength.

    ~or~

**CALL TO WORSHIP (Hebrews 12)**
    Where can we stand when God is shaking the earth?
        **We will stand on the promises of God.**
    Where can we find support when our foundations fail?
        **We will lean on the everlasting arms of God.**
    Where can we find salvation in times like these?
        **We will look to Jesus and to his covenant of life.**
    Let us worship the God of our salvation.

**OPENING PRAYER (Luke 13)**
    Great Healer, we are beaten down by life's suffering.
    Make us whole, O God,
        and help us share your healing with the world.
    Free us from the demons that shackle our spirits,
        and set us free from the chains that binds us,
            that we may help break the chains of others.
    Amen.

# PROCLAMATION AND RESPONSE

*PRAYER OF YEARNING (Jeremiah 1)*
Eternal God, you knew us before we were conceived.
You called us as your own
while we were still in our mothers' wombs.
Keep watch over us, we pray,
for we long to return to your ways.
Restore our confidence in times of doubt,
for we yearn to be the people you would have us be.
Grant us the confidence to go forth unafraid,
that we might bless the world
through your presence in our lives. Amen.

*ASSURANCE OF PARDON (Jeremiah 1)*
Touch our mouths to speak your truths.
Touch our lives to make your ways known to the world.
In this we are free.
In this we are made whole.
In this we shine as your beloved children,
strengthened for the journey.

*PASSING THE PEACE OF CHRIST*
God is our refuge and our strength, the very foundation
of our lives. Rest in this knowledge and share the joy of
God's love as you exchange signs of Christ's peace with
one another.

*RESPONSE TO THE WORD (Jeremiah 1, Psalm 71,*
*Hebrews 12)*
The Spirit has called us. Will we listen?
**We will heed the Spirit in our lives.**
God has a Word for us to share. Will we respond?
**We will share the words of the Lord.**
Christ has called us as disciples. Will we commit?
**We will live as disciples of our Lord and friend.**

# THANKSGIVING AND COMMUNION

### OFFERING PRAYER (Psalm 71, Hebrews 12)
God of power and might, in times of trial,
    you are our fortress and our refuge.
In thanksgiving and praise for your wonderful gifts,
    we offer you our tithes and offerings,
        that others might know the strength
            of your unshakable kingdom. Amen.

# SENDING FORTH

### BENEDICTION (Jeremiah 1, Luke 13)
God has set us free.
    **God releases us from bondage.**
Christ has made us whole.
    **Christ heals our wounds.**
The Spirit has strengthened us for the journey.
    **God's Spirit sends us forth.**
Go with the confidence of God's anointed.

~or~

### BENEDICTION (Luke 13)
God has set us free.
Christ has brought us peace.
The Spirit has made us whole.
Go with God.

Notes

# August 31, 2025

## Twelfth Sunday after Pentecost
## Proper 17

B. J. Beu
*Copyright © B. J. Beu*

## COLOR

Green

## SCRIPTURE READINGS

Jeremiah 2:4-13; Psalm 81:1,10-16;
Hebrews 13:1-8, 15-16; Luke 14:1, 7-14

## THEME IDEAS

Today's scriptures depict the pathos of a God who only wants good things for God's people. Time and again, we forsake living water for cracked cisterns that hold no water. We defile the very land God has given us for our fulfillment. Our religious leaders do not know the laws of life, and our rulers transgress against the Lord. We seek the seats of honor rather than looking to the needs of others. How long will we neglect to show hospitality to strangers? How many times will we fail to see the angels in our midst who seek to bless us? God's pathos flows from these passages. Will we listen? Will we hear? Will we honor the One who seeks our welfare?

# INVITATION AND GATHERING

*CENTERING WORDS (Jeremiah 2, Psalm 81)*
God calls us into fullness of life. Will we listen? Will we
hear? Will we honor the One who seeks our welfare?

*CALL TO WORSHIP (Jeremiah 2, Psalm 81)*
Sing in exaltation, people of God.
**The Lord fills us with good things.**
Shout for joy, children of the Holy One.
**God feeds us with finest wheat.**
God satisfies us with the sweetest honey.
**The Lord sustains us with living water.**

*OPENING PRAYER (Hebrews 13)*
Help us show hospitality to strangers, Merciful One,
    for many have entertained angels unaware
        while doing so.
Move us to treat one another
    as we would have others treat us,
        lest we find ourselves tortured or imprisoned
            with no one to come to our aid.
May we always seek to do good
    and share from our abundance,
        for these things are pleasing in your sight.
In your holy name, we pray. Amen.

# PROCLAMATION AND RESPONSE

*PRAYER OF YEARNING (Jeremiah 2, Psalm 81)*
Long-suffering One, we long to return to you
    with love and gratitude in our hearts.
We yearn for food that satisfies,
    the bread of life you offer without cost.

Refresh us from your living waters,
as we stare into the cracked cisterns
and the dry riverbeds of our petty complaints.
Stand by us, Holy One,
lest we forsake your glory in vain pursuits
that neither profit us nor bring us joy. Amen.

*WORDS OF ASSURANCE (Psalm 81:10, Hebrews 13:5)*
God offers us these words and this hope:
"I am the Lord your God,
who brought you up out of the land of Egypt.
Open your mouth wide and I will fill it."
God offers us these words of assurance:
"I will never leave you or forsake you."
God is faithful, even when we are not.

*PASSING THE PEACE (Jeremiah 2)*
We worship the One who brings us living water when
look to cracked cisterns. In gratitude and joy for God's
gracious gifts, let us share signs of the blessed peace we
find in Christ, our Lord.

*RESPONSE TO THE WORD (Psalm 81)*
Sing praises to God.
**Praise the One who offers us food
that truly satisfies.**
God gives us choicest bread and sweetest honey.
**We will laugh and play in the wellspring
of God's salvation.**

# THANKSGIVING AND COMMUNION

*OFFERING PRAYER (Jeremiah 2, Psalm 81, Luke 14)*
You free us, O God, from self-interest and folly.
You bring us into a land of choicest wheat
and sweetest honey.

As we return a portion of these gifts to you,
may we extend the banquet of your love to all—
especially the poor, the crippled, the lame,
the blind, and all who suffer.
May our offering bring healing and light
to a world filled with anguish and despair. Amen.

## SENDING FORTH

*BENEDICTION (Hebrews 13)*
Let mutual love continue,
that peace may abound.
Let mutual love flourish,
that God may be found.
Let mutual love grow,
that no one may feel forsaken.
Let mutual love abide,
that the hand of friendship may bless our world.

**Notes**

# September 7, 2025

## Thirteenth Sunday after Pentecost
## Proper 18

### Mary Scifres

## COLOR

Green

## SCRIPTURE READINGS

Jeremiah 18:1-11; Psalm 139:1-6, 13-18; Philemon 1-21;
Luke 14:25-33

## THEME IDEAS

The high price of following God emerges as a theme in today's scripture readings. This is particularly notable in Jesus' challenging lessons in Luke 14, and in Paul's command in Philemon to forgive and receive the escaped slave Onesimus as a beloved brother. Still, their messages echo what their Hebrew ancestors learned from Moses and the prophets. Following God is not for the faint of heart. Jeremiah and the psalmist remind us that when we go astray, the results can be disastrous. But hope remains that our Creator God, who crafted us from the beginning, can re-form us and put us back together again. Even though the cost of discipleship is high, the rewards of God's love are even greater.

# INVITATION AND GATHERING

*CENTERING WORDS (Jeremiah 18, Psalm 139, Luke 14)*
God knows us better than anyone and loves us more deeply than we can fathom. Even when we become less than God created us to be, God continues to love us and have faith in us.

*CALL TO WORSHIP (Jeremiah 18, Psalm 139, Luke 14)*
Did you hear the whisper of God calling us to worship?
**God, help us listen as you call.**
Do you sense the beautiful people
God is creating us to become?
**God, help us to see your image within.**
Are we ready to listen, learn, and grow?
**God, open our hearts and minds**
**to your loving and challenging guidance.**

*OPENING PRAYER or PRAYER OF YEARNING*
*(Jeremiah 18, Psalm 139, Luke 14)*
Creator God, you have crafted us in your image
and created us for greatness,
as we share your love, justice, and compassion.
Help us to live into this creation.
Strengthen us, as we seek to answer your call.
When we go astray,
guide us back to your ways.
When we fall apart,
put us back together again.
When we shrink in fear, lift our heads,
that we may see your love and grace
welcoming us home. Amen.

# PROCLAMATION AND RESPONSE

*PRAYER OF YEARNING (Psalm 139, Philemon 1)*
O God, you know us when we are at our very best
and when we are at our very worst.
So, here we are, ready to worship.
We are a confusing mixture of our best
and worst parts.
Thank you for inviting us here.
Thank you for always welcoming us home.
We welcome you, Holy Spirit.
Breathe in our lives,
as we worship you this day.
Be with us, now and always. Amen.

*WORDS OF ASSURANCE (Jeremiah 18, Psalm 139,
2 Corinthians 5)*
Marvelously set apart,
we are created in God's own image.
Marvelously saved by grace,
we are re-created in Christ's love.
Marvelously sustained in faith,
we are new creations in the Spirit.
Thanks be to God!

*PASSING THE PEACE OF CHRIST (Philemon 1)*
Let's welcome one another, not as strangers or even
friends, but as beloved sisters and brothers in Christ.

*INTRODUCTION TO THE WORD (Psalm 139)*
God's plans may be incomprehensible, but God's word
is not. Okay, sometimes it seems like it is. But let's give
it a try. Let's open our hearts and minds to what God
may be offering us today, trusting that God will speak
the truths we most need to hear.

### RESPONSE TO THE WORD (*Philemon 1, Luke 14*)
Carrying the cross may mean taking steps
  that frighten us.
Carrying the cross may mean listening
  instead of talking.
Carrying the cross may mean bringing love
  to the loveless.
Carrying the cross may mean confessing
  when we're embarrassed.
Carrying the cross may mean offering forgiveness
  to those who have hurt us.
Carrying the cross may mean sharing
  when we really don't want to.
Carrying the cross may mean . . . .
Take a moment of silence to reflect
  what carrying the cross might mean in your lives.

*(Time of Silence)*

Courageous Christ, help us to carry the cross,
  in ways that help us grow in love for you,
    for ourselves, and for the world. Amen.

# THANKSGIVING AND COMMUNION

### INVITATION TO THE OFFERING
Created by God to give and to share, let's give and share
with love and generosity, not just in this time of offering,
but in the days and weeks ahead.

### OFFERING PRAYER (*Psalm 139*)
Gracious God, you have blessed us beyond measure;
  you have entrusted us as partners
    to care for your world.
Bless these gifts and our very lives.

Transform everything we are in this life
    into offerings that bring your love to the world.
Amen.

## *INVITATION TO COMMUNION (Psalm 139)*
God, who knows the inmost parts of our being,
    invites all of us to this table of grace.
Come, all are welcome to Christ's banquet of love.

## *PRAYER OF CONSECRATION (Jeremiah 18, Psalm 139)*
Pour out your Holy Spirit
    on these gifts of bread and wine.
May they be your creative presence in our midst,
    your gracious love in our lives,
        and your eternal life for our salvation.
Breathe through each of us,
    and through this gathering,
        with the gifts of your Holy Spirit
Bring the breath of your love and grace to our world,
    that all may be created and redeemed by your grace
        and unified by your presence;
    and that all may be one in ministry with you,
        with one another, and with the world.
**Amen.**

# SENDING FORTH

## *BENEDICTION (Psalm 139, Luke 14)*
May the Spirit's power give us courage.
May Christ's love give us compassion.
And may God's image shine through us,
    as we carry a cross of light and love for all to see.
Amen.

# Notes

# September 14, 2025

## Fourteenth Sunday after Pentecost
## Proper 19

Silvia Purdie

## COLOR

Green

## SCRIPTURE READINGS

Jeremiah 4:11-12, 22-28; Psalm 14; 1 Timothy 1:12-17;
Luke 15:1-10

## THEME IDEAS

The story of the lost sheep has become a paradigm for
both faith and mission—faith from the perspective of
the sheep, and mission from the perspective of the shepherd. Countless stained glass windows show a lost lamb
in Christ's arms, and we value the experience of being
held, being saved, and being a beloved child. We are re-
minded of our lostness and need. But Paul calls us to
grow beyond this, through the outflow of mercy, and to
reach out to others. Each of us is also a shepherd. Mission calls us beyond victim-rescuer relationships into
mutual partnership, where we value the perspectives of
those who have wandered outside our comfort zones.

Can we hear the prophetic warnings of Jeremiah? Can we bring courage to the crises we face?

# INVITATION AND GATHERING

## CENTERING WORDS (Luke 15)

Jesus, the Good Shepherd, knows us and seeks us out.
Great is our joy as we are found in Christ.

## CALL TO WORSHIP (Psalm 14)

"There is no God!" people say.
  **"I can do what I like!" everyone thinks.**
"Who cares about God?" questioners ask.
  **"I'm here for me; I don't answer to anyone!"**
  **the foolish think.**
God looks for faith.
  **Will God find it?**
God looks for care of the poor.
  **Will we provide it?**
God looks for love.
  **Will God find it in us?**

## OPENING PRAYER (Psalm 14, Luke 15)

O God of heaven and earth,
  bless us with your mercy and grace.
Enter our hearts and make us holy.
Be our Shepherd and guide us in your ways,
  that we might not wander alone.
Hear our cries and gather us to yourself,
  that we may be one with each other,
    through the power of your Holy Spirit.
Amen.
(B. J. Beu)
Copyright © B. J. Beu

210

~or~

*OPENING PRAYER (Jeremiah 4, Psalm 14)*
God of wind and fire,
blow through our lives.
Release us from all that binds us,
and free us from thoughts the fears
that keep us from union with you
and with one another.
Lay waste to the burdens that impede us,
and wash away the debris that weighs us down.
As we strive to follow your path,
guide us onto the road of the righteous.
Make us of a refuge to the poor,
a deliverer to the captives,
and a friend to those who dwell alone.
In hope of your mercy, we pray. Amen.
*(B. J. Beu)*
*Copyright © B. J. Beu*

# PROCLAMATION AND RESPONSE

*PRAYER OF YEARNING (Psalm 14, Luke 15)*
God of heaven and earth, be with us in our need.
Though we often go astray,
we seek your love and mercy.
Though we often listen to fools who say,
"There is no God,"
our hearts belong to you.
Be our Shepherd and guide our ways,
for we are lost and afraid
and weary of wandering.
We long to be welcomed home
in your gracious mercy. Amen.
*(B. J. Beu)*
*Copyright © B. J. Beu*

### WORDS OF ASSURANCE

Thank you, King of the ages, for coming to us.
Thank you for loving us with utmost patience
  and for fitting us in your glory. Amen.

### PASSING THE PEACE OF CHRIST

Friends, God rejoices in you. For you were lost but now
are found. Let us share the peace of Christ and rejoice
that each and every one of us is highly treasured.

# THANKSGIVING AND COMMUNION

### OFFERING PRAYER

Most gracious God, we bring these gifts,
  as we bring ourselves.
We are nothing special in ourselves.
But you seek us, you gather us together;
  and in your arms, our lives come together.
Bless us and these gifts,
  that together we may be a blessing
    and return your glory to you,
      where it belongs. Amen.

### COMMUNION LITURGY (Luke 15)

Here we are, Lord—
  friends and strangers.
We are here to be your body.
We are here because you came to find us.
We were lost, but now are found.
Grace is here, more than enough to gather up
  the splintered pieces of our lives,
  the lost pieces gathered together
    in the hands of Jesus.
He is our savior,
  breaking bread, pouring wine,
  pouring out his very life blood in passion for us.

Mercy is here, overflowing with faith and love
    that are ours in Christ.
Power is here, surrendered and made whole.
Spirit is here, infusing these tangible things,
    forming us as community.
We belong to one another,
    because we belong to Christ.
Come, people of God.
We are all sinners and saints.
We are all lost and found.
Come to this table of grace and share in Christ,
    the Lamb and the Good Shepherd.

# SENDING FORTH

*BENEDICTION*
    Like a lost sheep, you are found by the Good Shepherd.
    Like a lost coin, you are gathered up by God.
    Be a good shepherd to those who are lonely.
    Be a good home for those longing to belong.
    Go in the untiring goodness of God,
        the unending patience of Christ,
        and the infinite peace of the Holy Spirit.
    Amen.

# Notes

# September 21, 2025

## Fifteenth Sunday after Pentecost
## Proper 20

### Michael Beu
*Copyright © Michael Beu*

## COLOR

Green

## SCRIPTURE READINGS

Jeremiah 8:18–9:1; Psalm 79:1-9; 1 Timothy 2:1-7; Luke 16:1-13

## THEME IDEAS

While Jeremiah and the psalmist cry out to God amid Israel's distress, we too can ease the plight of others. If a dishonest steward can earn Jesus' approval for being wise in earthly things, how much more approval will we receive for being wise in spiritual things? Proper management of our time, talents, and treasure matters.

# INVITATION AND GATHERING

### CENTERING WORDS (*Luke 16*)
Wisdom in matters of the Spirit gives us wings to fly.

**CALL TO WORSHIP** *(Jeremiah 8, Psalm 79)*
Search for the Lord each day.
**God waits where we least expect it.**
Search for the balm in Gilead.
**God brings healers in our need.**
Cry out to the Lord in times of distress.
**God comes speedily to meet us.**
Come! Worship the One who hears our pleas.

**OPENING PRAYER** *(Jeremiah 8, Psalm 79, 1 Timothy 2, Luke 16)*
Great Healer, be our balm of Gilead,
for we ache to be made whole.
Come to us in times of trial
and heal our sin-sick souls.
Amid those who prey on your little ones,
help us live faithfully as children of light.
May we be found faithful in a little,
that you may entrust us with much. Amen.

# PROCLAMATION AND RESPONSE

**PRAYER OF YEARNING** *(Jeremiah 8:22, Psalm 79)*
Why do you stay silent when scoffers say,
"Is there no balm in Gilead?
Is there no physician there?"
Your people need you, Merciful One.
We need you.
Our souls are wellsprings of sorrow
and we have shed rivers of tears.
Revive our souls, God of our salvation,
for in you alone do we renew our strength.
Come speedily to us once more
and reveal your glory to us,
that we find where our true help lies. Amen.

**ASSURANCE OF PARDON** *(Jeremiah 8, Psalm 79)*
> Know that there is a balm in Gilead
>> to heal the sin-sick soul.
> Rejoice and be glad,
>> for God's compassion comes speedily to meet us.

**PASSING THE PEACE OF CHRIST** *(1 Timothy 2)*
> Christ's peace is found in hearts that are turned to God.
> Let us find deep and abiding peace, as we share a moment of grace with one another.

**RESPONSE TO THE WORD** *(Luke 16)*
> We find true riches through faithfulness.
> We discover how to live as children of light
>> through lives of service.
> May we be faithful in what we have received,
>> that God may bless our work to bring God's realm
>> here on earth.

# THANKSGIVING AND COMMUNION

**OFFERING PRAYER** *(Luke 16)*
> You call us to be wise with our riches, O God,
>> that your realm may be blessed
>>> for the benefit of all.
> May we be found faithful in a little,
>> that you may entrust us to be faithful in much.
> We offer you these gifts
>> in gratitude for your love.
> May they bring your healing and light
>> to those who need the balm of Gilead. Amen.

# SENDING FORTH

**BENEDICTION** (*Luke 16*)
Be faithful in a little,
    that God may entrust you to be faithful in much.
Be faithful in much,
    that God may entrust you with the true riches
    that come from above.
Go as children of light,
    that you may know the grace, hope, and peace
    of the One who is truly faithful.

Notes

# September 28, 2025

## Sixteenth Sunday after Pentecost
## Proper 21

### B. J. Beu
Copyright © B. J. Beu

## COLOR

Green

## SCRIPTURE READINGS

Jeremiah 32:1-3a, 6-15; Psalm 91:1-6, 14-16;
1 Timothy 6:6-19; Luke 16:19-31

## THEME IDEAS

Today's Hebrew Scripture readings show the fulfillment of God's promises: return from exile, hope of new beginnings, and the assurance of new life springing from the ground. The New Testament readings focus on the trappings of wealth and the temptation to put our trust in money, rather than in God. Those who are wealthy have a responsibility to share their riches with the poor, for wealth is an opportunity to perform works of generosity. Paul and Jesus warn that hording our riches has eternal consequences.

# INVITATION AND GATHERING

### CENTERING WORDS (*Jeremiah 32, Psalm 91*)

God's promises are sure. We return from exile to find hope and new beginnings.

### CALL TO WORSHIP (*Psalm 91*)

God is our refuge and our fortress.
**In God, we place our trust.**
When we are weary,
**God lifts us up on wings like eagles.**
Come before the Lord with joy and longing.
**God is our hope and our salvation.**

### OPENING PRAYER or INVITATION TO THE OFFERING (*1 Timothy 6, Luke 16*)

Generous Spirit, you call us to share our riches
with the poor and disadvantaged,
lest we follow self-interest
to our ruin and destruction.
Teach us to bestow your blessings
on those in need,
lest we be trapped by selfish desire.
Set our hearts on the riches of good works,
rather than the allure of earthly treasures.
Help us take hold of the life that really is life. Amen.

# PROCLAMATION AND RESPONSE

### PRAYER OF YEARNING (*1 Timothy 6*)

Merciful God, in our quest for riches and success,
we often wander away from your ways
and pierce ourselves with many pains.
We yearn to be content with what we have,
for we brought nothing into this world
and take nothing from it when we leave.

We long to focus on things that endure:
    righteousness, godliness, faith, love,
        and gentleness.
Help us fight the good fight,
    that we might taste the sweetness of your salvation
        and touch the glory of eternal life in your name.
Amen.

*ASSURANCE OF PARDON (Psalm 91)*
    All who love the Lord, God will deliver.
    All who call on the Lord, God will answer.
    God satisfies the faithful with long life
        and the blessings of salvation.

*PASSING THE PEACE OF CHRIST*
    Having set our hearts on things that are above, let us
    share our joy with one another by exchanging signs of
    Christ's peace.

*RESPONSE TO THE WORD (Psalm 91)*
    Live in the shelter of the Most High.
    **Rest in the shadow of the Almighty.**
    Soar upon the wings of God's love.
    **Abide in the safety of Jesus' arms.**

# THANKSGIVING AND COMMUNION

*OFFERING PRAYER (Psalm 91)*
    Loving God, you protect us from harm
        and shelter us in your loving arms.
    Just as you deliver us from evil,
        may these offerings lead others
            to find the hope of your salvation.
    In Jesus' name, we pray. Amen.

# SENDING FORTH

**BENEDICTION (1 Timothy 6)**
Go with the promise of eternal life.
**We will live by faith.**
Go with the promise of heavenly riches.
**We will hold onto God's promises.**
Go and be rich in good works.
**We will be generous friends and neighbors.**
Go with God's blessings.

~or~

**BENEDICTION (Psalm 91, 1 Timothy 6)**
Dwell in the shelter of the Most High.
**In the shadow of the Almighty,
we rest secure.**
Fly above the storm upon the wings of God's love.
**In the unapproachable light of the living God,
we do not fear the shadow of death.**
With the blessings of our hope and our salvation,
**we will take hold of the life that really is life.**

# October 5, 2025

## Seventeenth Sunday after Pentecost
## World Communion Sunday
## Proper 22

### Leigh Anne Taylor

## COLOR

Green or White

## SCRIPTURE READINGS

Lamentations 1:1-6; Psalm 137; 2 Timothy 1:1-14;
Luke 17:5-10

## THEME IDEAS

Suffering and faith are at the heart today's readings for
World Communion Sunday. In Lamentations, we hear
the mourning of God's beloved, as they suffer the consequences of having betrayed their love for God and entrusted their lives to other gods. In Psalm 137, we hear
the enraged suffering of God's beloved, as they process
their unspeakable losses and pledge a renewed alle-
giance to God in exile. In Paul's letter to Timothy, we
hear a paradoxical "no fear, no shame" invitation to suffering, for the sake of the gospel of Christ Jesus. To enter
this suffering, Paul encourages Timothy to have faith in

God and to entrust his life to God, as he has. Timothy is to trust the power of the Holy Spirit in him. In Luke, the disciples ask Jesus to increase their faith, and he reminds them what God can do with even the little faith they have.

# INVITATION AND GATHERING

**CENTERING WORDS** *(Lamentations 1, Psalm 137)*
Where do you see human suffering? How might you participate in World Communion Sunday in solidarity with those who suffer?

**CALL TO WORSHIP** *(2 Timothy 1)*
The Holy Spirit rekindles God's purpose
and grace for our lives.
**Grace was given to us in Christ Jesus**
**before the ages began.**
Christ Jesus, our savior, abolished death
and brought life and immortality to light.
**This is good news, not just for ourselves,**
**but for the world.**
Let us worship in thanksgiving and praise.

**OPENING PRAYER** *(Lamentations 1, Psalm 137,*
*2 Timothy 1, Luke 17)*
Holy and Triune God,
your table transcends time and space.
As your disciples on World Communion Sunday,
we join our voices to the songs and prayers
offered to your name throughout the world.
Increase our faith and give us grace
to love and forgive one another,
as you have loved and forgiven us.

We remember all your beloved children
 who suffer this day—
  especially the victims and refugees of war.
We hear the echo of their broken lives
 in the songs of lament in today's scriptures.
Help us bear witness to their suffering without fear.
Give us the courage to live in love with you,
 in you, and for you.
For the sake of all your beloved children, we pray.
Amen.

# PROCLAMATION AND RESPONSE

## PRAYER OF YEARNING (2 Timothy 1)

Holy God, we need the witness of Timothy
 and the disciples,
  because we know what it is like—
   to be short on faith,
*(silent reflection)*
   to be afraid of failure,
*(silent reflection)*
   and to avoid suffering.
*(silent reflection)*
Holy God, we yearn for the encouragement
 of Paul and Jesus,
  because you still do mighty works
   through our tiny windows of faith.
*(silent reflection)*
Your holy call on our lives depends on your grace,
 not our success.
*(silent reflection)*
And your Holy Spirit gives us power
 to endure the suffering of our failures.
*(silent reflection)*

*WORDS OF ASSURANCE (2 Timothy 1)*
Rest assured, God has saved us from the endless cycle
of hatred and death-dealing—
things we too often do when left to our own devices.
**Thanks be to God for bringing us light and life,
through the saving love of Jesus Christ.**

*PASSING THE PEACE OF CHRIST (2 Timothy 1)*
Let's greet one another in Christian love:
**Grace, mercy, and peace:
from God, the Father;
from Christ Jesus, the Son;
and from the Holy Spirit.**

*RESPONSE TO THE WORD (2 Timothy 1)*
Light and life in Jesus Christ!
**Thanks be to God!**

# THANKSGIVING AND COMMUNION

*OFFERING PRAYER (Luke 17)*
Divine Master, purify the motivations of our hearts,
as we offer you the works of our hands.
May we work tirelessly,
until your servants can confidently say,
"We have done only what was ours to do."
May these gifts inspire us
to be as generous in our giving
and with our forgiveness,
as you have been with us. Amen.

# SENDING FORTH

**BENEDICTION (2 Timothy 1)**
Whether we are called to suffer little or to suffer much,
**we live in the faith and love**
**that are ours in Christ Jesus.**
Go in faith; go in love; go in God's power.
**With the help of the Holy Spirit alive in us,**
**we go in joy to bless our world.**

Notes

# October 12, 2025

## Eighteenth Sunday after Pentecost
## Proper 23

### Karin Ellis

## COLOR

Green

## SCRIPTURE READINGS

Jeremiah 29:1, 4-7; Psalm 66:1-12; 2 Timothy 2:8-15;
Luke 17:11-19

## THEME IDEAS

Today's scriptures focus on life—the abundant life God wants for each person, no matter where they are. Jeremiah sends a message to the exiles telling them that God wants them to thrive right where they are: build homes, tend the land, prosper, seek the welfare of the city, and pray. This message continues as the psalmist sings the glory of God and acknowledges that it is God who protects the people and blesses them. In the Epistle and the Gospel lessons, we see how life with God is carried on in the life and message of Jesus Christ. Second Timothy urges us to align themselves with Jesus Christ, knowing that Christ is always faithful. And Luke recounts the story of how Jesus brought healing and new life to ten lepers, but how only one returned to give thanks to Jesus. May we all strive to find the abundant life God offers through Jesus Christ.

# INVITATION AND GATHERING

### CENTERING WORDS (Jeremiah 29, 2 Timothy 2)

The Spirit invites us to deepen our faith in Christ and to find renewal and strength, by seeking the welfare of the community around us.

### CALL TO WORSHIP (Psalm 66)

People of Faith, come and see what God has done!
**God has guided us and walked with us.**
See how God has protected us.
**God has brought us to this sacred space.**
Let us give glory to God!
**Let us sing praises to God!**

### OPENING PRAYER (Psalm 66, 2 Timothy, Luke 17)

Holy One, we gather to sing your praises!
We are grateful for the gift of this day
and all the ways you make your presence known.
We are grateful for your abiding Spirit
and the ways the Spirit empowers us
to be your people.
In this time or worship, deepen our faith.
Restore our souls and heal us.
After we have spent time with you,
return us to our community,
that we may share your love and grace
with everyone we meet.
In the name of Christ, we pray. Amen.

# PROCLAMATION AND RESPONSE

*PRAYER OF CONFESSION (Jeremiah 29, 2 Timothy 2)*
>Gracious God, there are times in our lives
>>when we turn away from you,
>>when we mess up,
>>when we push aside the needs of our community,
>>>and when we ignore your presence in our lives.
>It is during these times that we cry out,
>>"Have mercy on us!"
>In your loving, forgiving way,
>>you reach out to heal us, forgive us,
>>>and renew us.
>May your everlasting faith strengthen our resolve
>>to follow Christ's ways. Amen.

*WORDS OF ASSURANCE (Luke 17)*
>Brothers and sisters, siblings in Christ,
>>hear the words Jesus spoke to the leper:
>"Your faith has made you well."
>In the name of Christ, you are forgiven, renewed,
>>and loved.
>Thanks be to God!

*PASSING THE PEACE OF CHRIST (2 Timothy 2)*
>The living Christ is here with us!
>>**Praise be to God!**
>May the peace of Christ dwell deeply in our souls.
>>**We will share this peace**
>>**with the entire community.**
>Let us do so now.

**PRAYER OF PREPARATION** *(Psalm 66, Luke)*
O Lord, may the words that are spoken
proclaim your goods deeds,
tell the stories of your faithfulness,
and remind us how to live in your ways.
Amen.

**RESPONSE TO THE WORD** *(Jeremiah 29, Luke 17)*
God of life, as we give thanks to you,
empower us to go on our way
as your faithful disciples.
Call us anew to seek the good of our community,
proclaim healing in your name,
and share your good news. Amen.

# THANKSGIVING

**INVITATION TO THE OFFERING** *(Psalm 66)*
God has done amazing things in our lives! Now is the time to offer our gratitude for all the blessings we have received. With thanks and praise, let us offer our gifts to God.

**OFFERING PRAYER** *(Jeremiah 29, Luke 17)*
Gracious God, we come to say thank you
for all the ways you bring forth life
and health and renewal.
Bless these gifts,
that they may bring forth life and healing
in our community. Amen.

# SENDING FORTH

**BENEDICTION (Jeremiah 29, Luke 17)**
Brothers and sisters, siblings in Christ,
as you go from this place,
may your faith grow stronger,
**We will share the good news
of Christ's healing love
with the community.**
Go in peace. Amen.

Notes

# October 19, 2025

## Nineteenth Sunday after Pentecost
## Proper 24

### James Dollins

## COLOR

Green

## SCRIPTURE READINGS

Jeremiah 31:27-34; Psalm 119:97-104; 2 Timothy 3:14–4:5;
Luke 18:1-8

## THEME IDEAS

Christ came that we may have life and have it abundantly. May we pursue an abundant, just, and peace-filled life, as persistently as the widow sought justice from an unjust judge. Thankfully, as the prophet Jeremiah tells us, God's covenant, the way to abundant life, is written on our hearts. It is also embedded in God's law, according to the psalmist. Let us persevere with God's help and not grow weary of seeking the goodness of God.

# INVITATION AND GATHERING

**CENTERING WORDS** *(Jeremiah 31, Luke 18)*
God's promises are written on our hearts. Look within,
recall them, and claim God's future of peace.

**CALL TO WORSHIP** *(Psalm 119)*
Oh, how I love your will, dear Lord.
I mediate on your wisdom all day long.
**Your teaching makes me wiser each day.**
**Your instruction helps me become my truest self.**
How sweet are your words to my taste,
sweeter than honey to my mouth.
**Your word is a lamp to my feet**
**and a light that shines on my path.**

**OPENING PRAYER** *(Luke 18)*
Come, Holy Spirit, and renew us
in this hour of celebration.
We rejoice that you make us your partners
in pursuit of a just and peaceful world.
With Jesus, we ask the question,
"Will there be faith on earth?"
Will we settle for mere beliefs,
or will we yield to the deep longing
for your will to be done, here and now?
Teach us to hope, work, and cry out
for your justice and peace to be made real.
Walk with us, Jesus, until we joyfully reach that day
when all God's children belong
to your eternal family. Amen.

# PROCLAMATION AND RESPONSE

### PRAYER OF CONFESSION or PRAYER OF YEARNING (Luke 18)

You call us, Lord of Life,
    to a faith that stays in motion.
You urge us to grow in wisdom
    and to be reconciled with all.
Yet, we fail to understand
    that faith is not something fixed
It is not a goal to be achieved,
    a place where we arrive
        and then rest on our laurels.
Call us anew, dear Christ,
    to seek you in neighbors who need us.
Help us pursue peace with more persistence
    than those who pursue violence.
Grant us an unyielding faith—
    a faith that transforms our own hearts
        and the world around us.
This we pray in your name, which is Love. Amen.

### WORDS OF ASSURANCE (Jeremiah 31)

"I will be your God, and you will be my people,"
    says the Lord.
God accepts us and calls us to accept all God's children.
In the name of Jesus Christ we are forgiven.
**In the name of Jesus Christ we are forgiven.
Amen.**

### RESPONSE TO THE WORD (Luke 18)

Do not puzzle over life's meaning or purpose.
God has told us what is good:
    **to do justice, love kindness,
    and walk humbly with our God.**

Let us cry out like the widow of Jesus' parable:
Grant us justice,
   **that creation may flourish free from harm.**
Grant us justice,
   **that vulnerable nations may live in peace.**
Grant us justice,
   **that differences between us**
   **will not limit anyone's opportunities.**
Grant us justice,
   **that all may be fed, housed, and healed.**
You invite us, dear Christ, to cry out for peace.
   **Walk with us, then, until we arrive at your side.**
   **Amen.**

*OFFERING PRAYER (Jeremiah 31)*
   Your promise is written on our hearts, dear God,
      and your strength is in the work of our hands.
   We offer you all that we have and all that we are,
      that your love may be made known
         throughout your world. Amen.

## SENDING FORTH

*BENEDICTION (Luke 18)*
   God's steadfast love never ceases.
   May we never fail to share this love with others.
   Go in the grace of Christ, the love of God,
      and the communion of the Spirit, now and always.
   Amen.

**Notes**

# October 26, 2025

## Twentieth Sunday after Pentecost
## Reformation Sunday
## Proper 25

### B. J. Beu
*Copyright © B. J. Beu*

## COLOR

Green

## SCRIPTURE READINGS

Joel 2:23-32; Psalm 65; 2 Timothy 4:6-8, 16-18;
Luke 18:9-14

## THEME IDEAS

God enters our struggles to bring us joy. In Joel, the Israelites are given life-giving rain after years of drought.
They also received the promise of prophecies, dreams,
and visions. The psalmist rejoices in the bounty of God's
blessings. Even as Paul contemplates his martyrdom, he
rejoices that he has finished the race in faith and will
receive the crown of righteousness. In Luke, Jesus chas-
tises those who build themselves up; but he offers forgiveness to those who humble themselves before God.
God never abandons us, especially in the worst of times.
This is good news indeed.

# INVITATION AND GATHERING

**CENTERING WORDS** *(Joel 2, Psalm 65, 2 Timothy 4)*
God dreams us into being. In turn, we dream God's dreams.

**CALL TO WORSHIP** *(Joel 2, Psalm 65)*
Rejoice in the Lord and be glad.
**God is our hope and our salvation.**
The Lord blesses the earth with rain.
**God crowns the year with bounty.**
The Lord makes old men dream dreams.
**God makes young girls see visions.**
Rejoice in the Lord and be glad.
**God is our hope and our salvation.**

**OPENING PRAYER** *(Joel 2, Psalm 65, 2 Timothy 4)*
Giver of dreams and visions,
pour out your Spirit on our fellowship,
for we need your presence in our lives.
Show your portents in the heavens
and set your signs on the earth and seas.
Touch our spirits with the awe of your majesty,
that we may humbly dwell within your courts
in peace and harmony. Amen.

# PROCLAMATION AND RESPONSE

**PRAYER OF YEARNING** *(Joel 2, Psalm 65, 2 Timothy 4)*
Merciful God, prepare us for the marathon of life,
even as seek the ease of a leisurely stroll.
May we never tire of fighting the good fight,
nor fall exhausted from running our race.
May we never grow weary from keeping the faith.

Speak your words of promise once more, O God,
    for we need to find your quiet center
        amid the noisy tumult of life.
Bless us with dreams and guide us with visions,
    that we may faithfully endure life's trials
        and receive your righteous crown. Amen.

*ASSURANCE OF PARDON (2 Timothy 4)*
    Christ offers a crown of righteousness
        to those who love him
        and long for his appearance.
    Rejoice and be glad!

*PASSING THE PEACE OF CHRIST (Joel 2)*
    With dreams and visions guiding our way, let us turn to
    one another and pass the peace of Christ.

*RESPONSE TO THE WORD (Ephesians 1, Acts 2)*
    God pours out the Holy Spirit on all flesh.
    **Our sons and our daughters shall prophesy.**
    Our old men and women shall dream dreams.
    **The young and old alike shall see visions.**
    Hold fast to the promises of God.
    **They are sure and true.**

# THANKSGIVING AND COMMUNION

*OFFERING PRAYER (Psalm 65, Luke 18)*
    God of overflowing abundance—
        you water the earth with live-giving rain;
        you clothe the meadows with glorious flowers;
        you deck the valleys with bountiful grain;
        you crown the year with your manifest blessings;
        you make the gateways of the evening
            and the morning shout for joy.

With what can we come before you?
How can we repay you for your grace and mercy?
Receive the fruit of our labor.
Receive also the gift of our humble thanks,
 and keep our hearts safe in your Spirit. Amen.

# SENDING FORTH

**BENEDICTION (2 Timothy 4)**
 Fight the good fight.
 Finish the race.
 Keep the faith.
 Love deeply and live well.
 Claim the crown of righteousness,
  which is given to all who love God
  and who yearn for Christ's appearance.

# Notes

243

# November 2, 2025

## Twenty-First Sunday after Pentecost
## All Saints Sunday

### B. J. Beu
*Copyright © B. J. Beu*

## COLOR

White

## SCRIPTURE READINGS

Daniel 7:1-3, 15-18; Psalm 149; Ephesians 1:11-23;
Luke 6:20-31

## THEME IDEAS

In the face of persecution and evil, God sustains the
faithful. God's blessings extend to the meek, the poor,
the hungry, and those who are persecuted for their faith.
God does not leave us comfortless, but offers us a glorious inheritance through Christ, who is seated at the
right hand of God. All Saints Day is a perfect occasion to
remember those who have died in the faith.

# INVITATION AND GATHERING

**CENTERING WORDS (Ephesians 1)**
In Christ we have a glorious inheritance through the power of the Holy Spirit. Let the saints of God rejoice!

**CALL TO WORSHIP (Psalm 149)**
Praise the Lord! Sing to the Lord a new song.
**Rejoice and be glad, for the Lord reigns.**
Praise God with dance.
**Praise God with songs of adoration.**
For God lifts up the lowly and casts down the mighty.
**Praise the Lord! Sing to the Lord a new song.**

~or~

**CALL TO WORSHIP (Daniel 7)**
When evil is afoot . . .
**God alone can save us.**
When nations rise against nation . . .
**God alone can set things right.**
When the innocent are devoured . . .
**God alone can heal our wounds.**
When our spirits are troubled . . .
**God alone can lead us home.**

**OPENING PRAYER (Ephesians 1, Luke 6)**
God of our forbearers, you turn our world upside down.
You teach us that neither wealth, nor social status,
nor reputation can lead us to life.
You remind us to focus on your kingdom,
where the poor, the hungry, the sorrowful,
and those persecuted for the gospel
receive your blessing.
Help us follow the example of the saints,
that we may receive our glorious inheritance,
by living as Christ taught us to live. Amen.

# PROCLAMATION AND RESPONSE

**PRAYER OF YEARNING (Luke 6)**
Spirit of Truth, feed our hearts
    from the fullness of your word.
We long to embrace the poor,
    who will inherit your kingdom.
We yearn to forsake the lure of earthly riches,
    lest we forestall your consolation.
Turn our failings into a fierce resolve to bear witness
    to the depth of your truth
        and the fullness of your grace. Amen.

**ASSURANCE OF PARDON (Ephesians 1)**
In Christ, we receive a glorious inheritance
    and God's redeeming grace.
Through the power of the Holy Spirit,
    we are sealed with the saints in holy love.

**RESPONSE TO THE WORD (Ephesians 1:13-14)**
You have heard the truth of the gospel
and the promise of our salvation.
    **Our hearts bear the seal of the Holy Spirit,**
    **which is our inheritance as God's people.**
Live as people redeemed and fitted for praise.

~or~

**RESPONSE TO THE WORD (Psalm 149)**
Praise the Lord!
    **Sing to the Lord a new song!**
Dance and sing before the Lord.
    **Praise the Lord with drum and guitar.**
Let the faithful rejoice in God's glory.
    **Praise the Lord!**

# THANKSGIVING AND COMMUNION

*OFFERING PRAYER (Psalm 149, Luke 6)*
God of abundant love, hear the songs of our hearts—
songs of thankfulness and praise,
songs of hope and expectation,
songs of laughter and joy,
songs of mirth and good will.
May our songs be sung throughout the world,
in the gifts we bring before you today.
May these melodies comfort those who weep,
bring mercy to the poor and imprisoned,
and offer encouragement to the weary. Amen.

# SENDING FORTH

*BENEDICTION (Psalm 149)*
God's love surrounds us.
**We go with God's blessing.**
God's joy lifts us.
**We go with God's blessing.**
God's hope nurtures us.
**We go with God's blessing.**

**Notes**

# November 9, 2025

## Twenty-Second Sunday after Pentecost
## Proper 27

### Michelle L. Torigian

## COLOR

Green

## SCRIPTURE READINGS

Haggai 1:15b–2:9; Psalm 145:1-5, 17-21;
2 Thessalonians 2:1-5, 13-17; Luke 20:27-38

## THEME IDEAS

The peace-filled Spirit of God is our great companion
on the journey, especially as our world trembles. Second
Thessalonians presents us with the vision that God is
our source of strength, comfort, and hope. As our foundation, God is near to us when we cry out in pain, anxiety, or confusion. Through faith, we know that God's
presence is steadfast, even when we don't know what
lies ahead, what tomorrow will bring, or how eternity
will appear.

# INVITATION AND GATHERING

## CENTERING PRAYER (Haggai 2, 2 Thessalonians 2)
No matter what is going on within and without, the
peace of God renews your cells and souls each moment.
In celebration of divine peace, inhale the refreshing serenity of the Spirit and exhale all that blocks you from
receiving the comforting love of Christ.

## CALL TO WORSHIP (Haggai 2, Psalm 145)
Inhale the bounty of God's peace.
**Splendor is a gift of the presence of God.**
Serenity is the treasure that comes from God's Spirit.
**Through the love of God, we find our rest.**
Now exhale all that resists the blessings of God.
**Justice and kindness ring from the heart of God.**

## OPENING PRAYER (Haggai 2, Psalm 145,
## 2 Thessalonians 2, Luke 20)
Divine Foundation, even as tumultuous winds shake us
　　and the floor beneath us quakes,
　　　　you firmly hold us.
As the world around us rattles,
　　you erase fear from our hearts.
Whether on earth or in heaven,
　　your loving Spirit endures.
It pervades the limitless reaches
　　of your creation.
Lift us during times of trembling, enduring Spirit,
　　and still us during moments of uncertainty. Amen.

# PROCLAMATION AND RESPONSE

*PRAYER OF CONFESSION (Haggai 2, Psalm 145,*
*2 Thessalonians 2)*
> Holy God, Sacred Serenity—
> the vibrations of our worry shake us to the core.
> We want answers now, not tomorrow.
> Our minds demand proof that all will be well.
> We refuse to wait with peace and patience for certainty.
> We blame ourselves for calamities,
>> even when they are beyond our control.
> We accuse you for mishaps,
>> even when your hand has only loved us.
> As the earth's roads crack below us,
>> your sacred foundation sturdies us.
> May your strength embolden us
>> in times of trouble and distress,
>>> that we may move forward with hope. Amen.

*WORDS OF ASSURANCE (Haggai 2, 2 Thessalonians 2)*
> Whether under moonlight or during the day,
>> the steadfast grace of God delivers us
>> from the shame stirring within us.
> May the eternal comfort and hope of our Creator
>> fill our hearts with peace and courage
>> for the road ahead.

*PASSING THE PEACE OF CHRIST (Psalm 145,*
*2 Thessalonians 2)*
> Living in the realm of the just and kind Holy One, may
> we build one another up, knowing that our strength
> comes from our Creator. Let us share these gifts with
> our siblings near and far.

*RESPONSE TO THE WORD (Psalm 145)*
Meditate on the Spirit of God.
**Celebrate the splendor of the Spirit's presence.**
Ponder the glorious works of our God.
**In poetry and song, our ancestors rejoiced
in God's love.**
Our voices will praise our wondrous Lord.
**And our hands will share God's steadfast mercy.**

# THANKSGIVING AND COMMUNION

*INVITATION TO OFFERING (Haggai 2, Psalm 145)*
Through the work of our hearts and hands, we are called to deliver the justice and kindness of God. Courage is our guide, as we discern which gifts to share. May the wisdom of God our Creator shine on our pathways along the way.

*OFFERING PRAYER (Haggai 2, Psalm 145,
2 Thessalonians 2)*
Holy, Steadfast Love, as we abide together in your realm,
    you bring stillness to our hurried world.
Even as the world quakes and our anxiety builds,
    your peace blesses our souls.
Help us share this serenity with our companions
    on the road.
Bless the gifts we return to you this day,
    that they may bring unity to your realm
        and hope for a harmonious universe. Amen.

# SENDING FORTH

**BENEDICTION** *(Haggai 2, Psalm 145, 2 Thessalonians 2, Luke 20)*

May the God of strength fill our hearts with hope,
as we face a quaking world.
May the Christ of love fill our hearts with faith,
as we wonder what's next.
May the Spirit of peace fill our hearts with tranquility,
as we seek eternal comfort.
May God's splendor illuminate the road ahead,
as we seek the joy of heaven. Amen.

Notes

# November 16, 2025

## Twenty-Third Sunday after Pentecost
## Proper 28

### Kirsten Linford

## COLOR

Green

## SCRIPTURE READINGS

Isaiah 65:17-25; Isaiah 12; 2 Thessalonians 3:6-13; Luke 21:5-19

## THEME IDEAS

Three of today's lections almost read as a single narrative. In Luke, we hear prophesies of fear and concern—destruction, signs, and persecutions. While some might hear these words in an apocalyptic context, they may be more useful when used to reflect the traumas, fears, and suffering we all face in life. The end of the passage, promising that the faithful will not perish, leads naturally into Isaiah 65 and its promise of new heavens and a new earth, joy that overcomes all weeping, and a peace beyond all imagination. Assured of new life, we can then hear Isaiah 12 as the response of the people to the goodness of God—as they speak of God's comfort and salvation and respond with deepest thanks and praise.

# INVITATION AND GATHERING

**CENTERING WORDS *(Isaiah 65, Luke 21)***

What suffering are we facing in our lives? How do we respond to the turmoil and voice around us? When we are most anxious, most afraid, can we hold onto the promise of God's new heavens and new earth? Can we let ourselves imagine the grace that may yet come?

**CALL TO WORSHIP *(Isaiah 65)***

I am about to create new heavens and a new earth.
**Thus says our God, the Holy One.**
Be glad and rejoice in this new creation.
**Celebrate all that is coming to you.**
For your weeping shall be met with rejoicing.
**And your suffering will be overtaken by new life.**
You shall build homes and live in them;
**plant gardens and eat from them.**
Whenever you call, I will answer.
**When you cry out, I will come.**
Heaven and earth will be filled with my peace.
**Everything will become a new creation.**

**OPENING PRAYER *(Isaiah 12, Luke 21)***

Loving and Merciful God, we give you thanks.
You bring us strength, when we feel weak;
courage, when we cannot stand.
You fill our hearts with your glory
and bless our being with your grace.
You protect our lives.
In your care, not one hair on our heads shall perish,
nor the smallest flutter of peace
perish in our souls. Amen.

# PROCLAMATION AND RESPONSE

**PRAYER OF YEARNING (Luke 21, 2 Thessalonians 3)**
O God, we want to be strong, but are often not.
We wish we could be unaffected by the world
    and give all our anxiety away.
And yet, we hold onto our worries and fears,
    as if they could bring us comfort,
        the way you do.
We want to be brave and have the courage
    to release the trappings of this world,
        to reach for something that is really real.
When the world falls apart around us;
    when we don't know where to start to heal it;
    when we turn to things that never satisfy,
        help us place our trust in you.
Keep our hearts from being idle
    and our souls from giving in to despair,
        for you are just waiting to bring new life. Amen.

**WORDS OF ASSURANCE (Isaiah 65, Isaiah 12)**
Loving One, you meet our fear with comfort,
    our anger with grace.
Just when we have convinced ourselves
    that you have forgotten us,
        we find you turning back, and back,
            and back to us.
Meet us with your salvation—
    a gift beyond what we have dared to ask.
Redeem our fears and turn them into joy.
Sing through us, O God,
    that we may have the voice and the peace
        to sing through you,
            forever and ever. Amen.

*PASSING THE PEACE OF CHRIST (Isaiah 65)*
We are offspring blessed by the Lord. So shall our descendants be. Let God's peace surround us and fill us, now and forever, as we share signs of peace and welcome.

*PRAYER OF PREPARATION (Psalm 19)*
May the words of my mouth . . .
**and the meditations of our hearts**
**be acceptable in your sight, O Lord,**
**our strength and our redeemer. Amen.**

*RESPONSE TO THE WORD (Isaiah 12)*
God's Word is a wellspring of our salvation.
Drink deep of its joy.
God's deeds have been made known to us.
God's love has drawn notice among all nations.
So, sing God's praises.
Shout your joy to the Holy One.
Give thanks to our God and call on God's name—
in this time and forevermore. Amen.

# THANKSGIVING AND COMMUNION

*INVITATION TO THE OFFERING (Isaiah 65)*
God has given us home and hearth and love without end. Let us share our lives and our gifts with the One who has gifted us.

*OFFERING PRAYER (Isaiah 65)*
Gracious God, you have given us new heavens
and a new earth.
You bless us with new life and presence,
more than ever before.

So, let us build and share our homes.
Let us plant gardens
    and offer the fruit to those who hunger.
We offer our gifts to you and to all your people.
For then shall we too be fed—
    in body and in spirit. Amen.

# SENDING FORTH

**BENEDICTION (Isaiah 65)**
People of God, the Lord calls.
    **We shall answer—**
    **embracing new life, blessed peace,**
    **and a love that has no end. Amen.**

# Notes

# November 23, 2025

## Reign of Christ/Christ the King Sunday
## Proper 29

Rebecca Gaudino

## COLOR

White

## SCRIPTURE READINGS

Jeremiah 23:1-6; Luke 1:68-79; Colossians 1:11-20;
Luke 23:33-43

## THEME IDEAS

Today's writers offer differing visions of God's reign in
human lives and situations. Jeremiah and Zechariah offer an elite priestly vision: a high-flown and patriarchal
vision of a dynastic king, also called a shepherd and
"horn of salvation" (the Greek behind "mighty savior"
in Luke 1:69, NRSVue). In this vision, power flows on
high to enable the Davidic ruler to "execute justice and
righteousness in the land" (Jeremiah 23:5). The letter to
the church in Colossae, however, speaks to everyday
men and women, as we see in the closing verses that re-
fer to Aristarchus and Onesimus as well as to Nympha
and her house church. The vision of God's work in these
early Christians' lives is of the divine presence that surrounds and enlivens each of their lives. For this early

Christian writer, the priority status of Jesus, his being "the beginning" of creation, of life beyond death, of the church, is not about a king ruling over us. The promise of Jesus is a presence that holds, embraces, strengthens, and gives us hope for the peace and reconciliation we long for in our human circumstances.

# INVITATION AND GATHERING

### CENTERING WORDS (Luke 1)
God shines holy light into the shadows of our world.
The sun of God's mercy and strength bathes all creation.

### CALL TO WORSHIP (Luke 1, Colossians 1)
Blessed be the Holy One,
**who looks upon us with love and mercy.**
Blessed be the Holy One,
**who sent us a Savior to rescue us from despair.**
Blessed be the Holy One and God's beloved Child,
**who rules in a realm of forgiveness and peace.**
Blessed be the Holy One,
**who is worthy of our worship.**

### OPENING PRAYER (Colossians 1)
God of Creation, we cannot see you,
but we see what you have created
in all its beauty and bounty!
Jesus, Child of God, the entire universe
lives in you, and for you, and through you!
Spirit of the Holy One, you sweep across creation,
enlivening and sustaining.
Everything on earth and in heaven
has its being and its hope because of you,
Triune God.
Blessed is your holy, life-giving name! Amen.

# PROCLAMATION AND RESPONSE

**PRAYER OF YEARNING (Colossians 1)**
Jesus, Beloved Child of God, in and through you,
    God brings all creation together for good.
We and our world need your peace.
Sometimes we are strong and able,
    standing without fear.
But sometimes we are weary and in distress,
    living in the shadows of disappointment
        and failure.
But you are our Deliverer.
In love and power, you hold the fullness of God;
    you bring the fullness of our lives and our world.
Surround us with your love and life
    and grant us your presence of peace.
In your powerful and loving name, we pray. Amen.

**WORDS OF ASSURANCE (Luke 1, Colossians 1)**
Through Jesus, our Savior, God is pleased
    to be reconciled to all things,
        on earth and in heaven.
Blessed be the Holy One, who redeems and saves us!

**PASSING THE PEACE OF CHRIST (Colossians 1)**
*(Colossians envisions Christ's rule as something that encompasses and envelops. Bring a large crown to worship. Hold up this crown as the traditional monarchical symbol of Christ's rule. But then turn the crown on its side to show the circle. Jesus is the one who surrounds, encircles, encompasses—a symbol of powerful embrace, a kind of power that could even be described as womblike.)*

Each of us dwells in the realm of God. Let us greet one another as friends and family in the peace of Jesus Christ!

*RESPONSE TO THE WORD (Colossians 1)*
Jesus Christ, Beloved Child of God,
you hold our lives and the lives of all we hold dear.
Within your very being,
you reconcile everything to yourself.
Nourish us and our world with your life-giving power,
that we might know hope and peace. Amen.

# THANKSGIVING AND COMMUNION

*OFFERING PRAYER (Colossians 1)*
Loving God, may our gifts bring your love to all.
Jesus Christ, our Deliverer,
may our gifts show the world
that we belong to one another.
For each of us is held in your embrace.
In the name of the Holy Spirit,
who gives the breath of life, we pray. Amen.

# SENDING FORTH

*BENEDICTION (Luke 1, Colossians 1)*
May God guide our feet in the way of peace!
**May we be strong in the strength
of God's glorious power!**
May we be joyful in the gifts we share
with all God's people!
**May we be at peace in Christ,
who encompasses all that is and will be!
Amen.**

# Notes

# November 27, 2025

## Thanksgiving Day

### Anna Crews Camphouse

## COLOR

Red

## SCRIPTURE READINGS

Deuteronomy 26:1-11; Psalm 100; Philippians 4:4-9;
John 6:25-35

## THEME IDEAS

The journey of life is filled with both joys and sorrows.
Yet, all things work together for the good of those who
love God and who are called according to God's purposes. As we wander through the deserts and valleys of
the spiritual life, finding manna in the wilderness, we
are called to release our anxieties and replace them with
an alignment of mind, body, and soul. We are called to
do God's will for our lives. Doing these ancient spiritual practices, with sincerity and trust, develops abiding
praise and thanksgiving.

# INVITATION AND GATHERING

**CENTERING WORDS (Philippians 4:4-9)**
*(Repeat these sentences silently to yourself to quiet your mind and open your heart.)*

I release my worries, anxieties, shoulds, and ought tos.
I prepare my mind, heart, body, and soul for the divine inbreaking of love and gratitude.

**CALL TO WORSHIP (Psalm 100)**
*(This liturgy aligns with the Kabbalistic diagram and/or chakras. If presented on a slideshow, using the colors red, orange, yellow, green, blue, indigo, and violet for each call and response would be appropriate.)*

We bring our thanksgiving for the earth,
our church, and our community.
**Make a joyful noise, singing praise**
**to God's everlasting goodness and mercy.**
We bring our gratitude for our families,
our children, and friends near and far.
**Make a joyful noise, singing praise**
**to God's everlasting goodness and mercy.**
We come into this worship with thanksgiving
for the purpose and God places on our lives
to serve, love, and give.
**Make a joyful noise, singing praise**
**to God's everlasting goodness and mercy.**
We come into this service with hearts filled with love
for Christ, ourselves, and our neighbors.
**Make a joyful noise, singing praise**
**to God's everlasting goodness and mercy.**
We enter into a relationship today with God's Spirit,
to make the best choices to fulfill our souls' mission.
**Make a joyful noise, singing praise**
**to God's everlasting goodness and mercy.**

We enter into a relationship with the mind of Christ,
offering every thought for transformation
into the holy joy of obedience and abundant life.
**Make a joyful noise, singing praise**
**to God's everlasting goodness and mercy.**
In wholeheartedness, we celebrate the gift of being one
with God, images of the divine creativity,
co-creating heaven on earth in the now
through the power and grace of your will and way.
**Make a joyful noise, singing praise**
**to God's everlasting goodness and mercy.**

*OPENING PRAYER (Psalm 100, Philippians 4)*
Giver of peace, our hearts and tongues praise you,
offering thanks for every season of life.
Your mercy, provision, and direction
have guided us through both storm and sunshine.
When the rains of fear, anxiety, and despair
fall upon our weary souls,
refocus our minds on things that are noble, right,
pure, lovely, admirable, and praiseworthy.
Make us channels of hope, as the hands of Christ.
In gratitude and peace, we pray. Amen.

# PROCLAMATION AND RESPONSE

*PRAYER OF YEARNING (Deuteronomy 26)*
Almighty God, maker of heaven and earth,
fill our hearts with gratitude
on this day of Thanksgiving.
You bring us into a land
flowing with milk and honey.
You bless us with waters
that well up to eternal life.

Open our mouths to proclaim your bounty,
> for by your power alone do we prosper.
Help us to live each day with true gratitude
> for your many blessings. Amen.
*(B. J. Beu)*
*Copyright © B. J. Beu*

## WORDS OF ASSURANCE (John 6)

God is indeed love.
God is with the wandering, the lost, the questioning,
> and those who feel unworthy.
God accepts you.
You are enough.

## PASSING THE PEACE OF CHRIST (Psalm 100, Philippians 4)

Take a slow, deep breath. Hold the air in your lungs and savor the oxygen you need to survive. Exhale the air, recognizing that every molecule is shared with everyone else here. Use the breath you share to speak words of peace and life to one another.

## PRAYER OF PREPARATION (Deuteronomy 26:1-11)

Crafter of the journey, calm our wandering minds
> and our anxious spirits.
Remembering your past faithfulness
> to those who have come before us,
>> we ask for the strength to embrace the path
>> you call us to walk this day.
We open our souls to your guidance,
> that we may give you all we have become
> and are still becoming,
>> as we follow the way of Jesus. Amen.

RESPONSE TO THE WORD *(Deuteronomy 26)*
God transforms our wandering into blessed direction.
Our wondering is being satiated by the gifts of Word,
worship, and wholeness.
Our wellness is birthing new life,
through the soulfulness of these moments.
Through it all, we give deep thanks to God,
the true north of our soul's path. Amen.

# THANKSGIVING AND COMMUNION

INVITATION TO THE OFFERING *(Deuteronomy 26)*
Come weary wanderer to the table of gifts
and offer your harvest to a needy world.
**We offer our first fruits, the best we have,**
**to the service of God and others.**
May God transform our hurt into joy and hope.
**May God transform our sorrow and despair**
**into divine ascendance.**

OFFERING PRAYER *(John 6)*
Baker of the bread of life, like desert wanderers of old,
we seek your manna.
We bring our gifts and offerings this day,
that the hope of the bread of heaven
might be manifested for all.
Ground us in the power of the eternal now
and satiate the physical, emotional,
and spiritual hunger within us. Amen.

INVITATION TO COMMUNION *(John 6)*
The bread of heaven is available to all.
Come and find nourishment for the soul's journey.
Come and partake of the abundant grace
and provision of God.

**GREAT THANKSGIVING** (*Deuteronomy 26, John 6*)
The Lord be with you.
**And also with you.**
Lift up your hearts.
**We lift them up to the Lord.**
Let us give thanks to the Lord our God.
**It is right to give our thanks and praise.**

It is right, and a good and joyful thing,
always and everywhere to give thanks to you,
our Great Provider, creator of heaven and earth.
In our wilderness days of wandering,
you provided manna for your people.
In our times, you work through the darkness
for our good.
In our self-imposed prisons
of poor choices and unenlightened mistakes,
you offer us a key to freedom,
providing comfort, friends, and support.
In our unscripted lives, you show up
and give us cues to know what to do next.
When we are famished for love and care,
you provide the bread of heaven
to restore our souls.

And so, with all your people on earth,
and all the company of heaven,
we praise your name and join their unending hymn:
**Holy, holy, holy Lord, God of power and might,**
**heaven and earth are full of your glory.**
**Hosanna in the highest. Blessed is the One**
**who comes in the name of the Lord.**
**Hosanna in the highest.**

Holy are you, and blessed is your Son, Jesus Christ,
    who showed us the depth of love incarnate
    and manifested healing, grace, and love
    in miraculous ways.
He showed us that the Spirit within him is ours, too.
He blessed us, that we might:
    create the heavenly realm here on earth;
    become living incarnations of God's love and grace;
    shine a light like a beautiful city on a hill;
    and become the beloved unified community
    God dreams us to be.

On the last night he had dinner with his closest friends,
    he took the bread, gave thanks to you,
    broke the bread, and gave it to his disciples, saying:
    "Take, eat. This is my body which is given for you.
    Do this in remembrance of me."
When the supper was over, he took the cup,
    gave thanks to you,
    and gave it to his disciples, saying:
    "Drink from this, all of you. This is my blood
    of the new covenant, poured out for you
    and for many for the forgiveness of sins.
    Do this, as often as you drink it,
    in remembrance of me."

And so, in remembrance of these,
    your beautiful and sacred acts in Jesus,
    we offer ourselves in praise and thanksgiving,
    a holy and living offering of hope and care,
    in union with Christ's offering and love for us,
    as we proclaim the mystery of faith.
    **Christ has died.**
    **Christ is risen.**
    **Christ will come again.**

**COMMUNION PRAYER**
Pour out the blessings and fullness of your Spirit
on all who gather at this table
and on these sacred symbols of bread and wine.
Infuse them with the essence of Christ,
that we may be the hands and feet of Christ
for a world in need.
By your Spirit, unite us with Christ and one another,
that we may be one in ministry,
in fullness and grace,
both in this life and the next.
Through your Son Jesus,
with the guidance and power of the Holy Spirit,
and through the connection and embodiment
of the Church,
all honor and glory is yours,
Creator and Source of all,
now and forever. Amen.

# SENDING FORTH

**BENEDICTION (Psalm 100, Philippians 4, John 6, Deuteronomy 26)**
The divine has already placed manna on your journey.
Embrace the bread of heaven in the eternal now,
which is present in every breath.
Know that angels guide your wandering.
And may the presence of the Spirit fill you,
flow through you, and become embodied in you,
as you incarnate God's love,
through thought, word, and action. Amen.

# Notes

# November 30, 2025

## First Sunday of Advent

### Mary Petrina Boyd

## COLOR

Purple

## SCRIPTURE READINGS

Isaiah 2:1-5; Psalm 122; Romans 13:11-14;
Matthew 24:36-44

## THEME IDEAS

Advent begins with a sense of preparation and urgent waiting. We prepare, but we don't know when, because time is in God's control. Let us live, then, with anticipation and readiness. Peace weaves through these scriptures: swords into plowshares, peace for Jerusalem, and peace from quarrels. We are called to put on Christ and walk in God's ways.

## INVITATION AND GATHERING

### CENTERING WORDS (Psalm 122)

God is here. There is peace and security in this place.

**CALL TO WORSHIP** *(Isaiah 2, Romans 13, Matthew 24)*
What time is it?
**This is God's time!**
What time is it?
**It is a time for peace.**
What time is it?
**It is a time to get ready.**
What time is it?
**It is time to worship and sing praise!**

~or~

**CALL TO WORSHIP** *(Isaiah 2, Romans 13)*
Come, let us walk in the light of the Lord.
**Let us enter God's presence.**
God will teach us the ways of peace.
**Let us travel along God's paths.**

~or~

**CALL TO WORSHIP** *(Isaiah 2, Romans 13)*
We begin the journey that leads to Christmas.
**Let us walk in the light of the Lord.**
This is a journey of peace.
**Let us beat swords into plowshares.**
This is a journey of hope.
**Let us walk with God.**

~or~

**CALL TO WORSHIP** *(Matthew 24)*
Wake up!
**Why?**
It's time!
**What time is it anyway?**
It's time to get ready for Jesus.
**Let's go and get ready!**

**OPENING PRAYER (Isaiah 2, Romans 13)**
>Everlasting God, we begin our journey
>>toward Christmas with hope stirring within.
>Teach us how to get ready.
>Show how to prepare our hearts for Jesus.
>Help us walk in your ways,
>>as we put on your Son, Jesus Christ.
>Guide us on your paths of peace and understanding,
>>as we prepare our hearts anew for the road ahead.
>Amen.

# PROCLAMATION AND RESPONSE

**PRAYER OF YEARNING (Isaiah 2, Romans 13, Matthew 24)**
>Holy One, we want to know your plan.
>We want to know when and how things will happen.
>You have shown us your ways
>>and taught us to walk in the paths of peace.
>Teach us to trust your never-ending care,
>>for our future is in your hands.
>Help us cast aside our holiday worries
>>and live with Advent joy! Amen.

**WORDS OF ASSURANCE (Psalm 122)**
>God offers us peace and security.
>God goes with us on our journey.

**PASSING THE PEACE OF CHRIST (Isaiah 2, Psalm 122, Romans 13)**
>God calls us to set aside our weapons, stop fighting, and live in peace and security.

~or~

**PASSING THE PEACE OF CHRIST** *(Isaiah 2, Psalm 122)*

Let us beat our swords into plowshares and our spears into pruning tools. God wants us to live in peace. Share this peace with one another.

**PRAYER OF PREPARATION** *(Romans 13)*

Slow us down, Lord.
Help us set aside our worries and concerns,
    our lists and our distractions.
Show us your ways,
    as we listen to your word.
Teach us and train our hearts, we pray. Amen.

**RESPONSE TO THE WORD** *(Isaiah 2, Matthew 24)*

God of the ages, we want to be ready for you.
But it is easy to be impatient as we wait.
Teach us to trust your time.
Help us rest secure,
    as we long for your promised peace.
Teach us to walk in your ways—
    ways that lead to peace. Amen.

# THANKSGIVING AND COMMUNION

**OFFERING PRAYER** *(Isaiah 2, Psalm 122)*

God of all goodness,
    as we walk in the light of your love,
        we are blessed by the abundance of your gifts.
You give us the beauty of nature,
    food to nourish our bodies,
        and communities to love and support us.
Out of our abundance,
    we bring our gifts to you.
May these gifts increase peace in our community
    and throughout the world. Amen.

# SENDING FORTH

## BENEDICTION (Isaiah 2, Psalm 122)
May peace be within your walls.
May security bless your homes.
And may serenity reside in your hearts.
Go to walk in the light of the Lord!

## Notes

# December 7, 2025

## Second Sunday of Advent

### Karin Ellis

## COLOR

Purple

## SCRIPTURE READINGS

Isaiah 11:1-10; Psalms 72:1-7, 18-19; Romans 15:4-13;
Matthew 3:1-12

## THEME IDEAS

On this Second Sunday of Advent, we catch a glimpse
of God's vision for a peaceable kingdom as we continue
to make our way to Bethlehem. The prophet Isaiah casts
a vision of a ruler, a child, who will bring such peace to
the earth that all creatures will live peacefully together and no one will destroy or hurt any part of creation.
Psalm 72 continues the theme of a ruler who will bring
God's justice and harmony to all. Paul, in his letter to
the Romans, tells the people that all are welcomed in the
name of Christ, and all are invited to give glory to God.
In Matthew, we hear the cries of John the Baptist, who
calls out in the wilderness, proclaiming one who will
bring God's righteousness and justice, God's peace and
hope. May this be a day when God's hope and peace is
proclaimed with great joy.

# INVITATION AND GATHERING

### CENTERING WORDS (Romans 15)

Lay down your burdens. Forget your fears. Christ has invited you here. live in the hope and peace of God.

### CALL TO WORSHIP (Psalm 72, Romans 15)

People of God, Christ has invited us here!
**We gather to praise God,**
**who brings justice and righteousness to all.**
We gather to give thanks to God for hope and peace.
**Blessed be the Lord,**
**who has done marvelous things.**
Let us praise God together!

### OPENING PRAYER (Isaiah 11, Romans 15, Matthew 3)

God of hope and peace, as we worship you this day,
may we catch a glimpse of your peace;
may we open ourselves to receive your grace;
may we welcome one another,
as you have welcomed us;
may we prepare hearts and our lives,
for Christ to be born in us once again.
And when our worship is done,
may we be renewed in body and spirit,
prepared to bring your righteousness and justice
to the world.
In the name of Christ, we pray. Amen.

# PROCLAMATION AND RESPONSE

*PRAYER OF CONFESSION (Isaiah 11, Matthew 3)*
> Merciful God, there are days when we lose our way.
> We forget, or simply don't trust, your vision of peace.
> We ignore the cries of those seeking justice.
> We fail to bear good fruit in our lives.
> Forgive us.
> Remind us that we are yours.
> Teach us how to make peace with ourselves
> > and with our neighbors.
> Help us proclaim your message of hope
> > and continue our journey to Bethlehem—
> > > a journey of faith to a cradle of love.
> In the name of Emmanuel, we pray. Amen.

*WORDS OF ASSURANCE (Romans 15)*
> Brothers and sisters, siblings in Christ,
> > the God of steadfast love encourages us
> > to continue in the faith.
> Rejoice, for God brings forgiveness and healing.
> Thanks be to God!

*PASSING THE PEACE OF CHRIST (Psalm 72)*
> Wherever you have been, you are welcome here!
> > **We are glad to be here,**
> > **gathered in the glorious name of God!**
> Here and everywhere, may the peace of Christ
> be with you.
> > **And also with you.**

*PRAYER OF PREPARATION (Isaiah 11)*
> Holy One, may your Spirit bring wisdom
> > and understanding to all people.
> May your Spirit guide and encourage us
> > to love you more deeply. Amen.

281

**RESPONSE TO THE WORD** *(Psalm 72 and Matthew 3)*
People of God, as we await the birth of Christ,
we are encouraged to bear good fruit.
**We will strive to share God's hope, peace,**
**righteousness, and justice with our community.**
May we all continue to bless God's holy name!
**Amen.**

# THANKSGIVING AND COMMUNION

**INVITATION TO THE OFFERING** *(Psalm 72)*
We give thanks for the blessings God gives us—blessings that nourish us and help us do wondrous things for God and God's world. In a spirit of thanksgiving, let us now offer what we can to God as a way to show our thanks.

**OFFERING PRAYER** *(Isaiah 11, Psalm 72, and Matthew 3)*
Abundant God, your blessings and righteousness
are bountiful in our lives.
May these gifts bear good fruit as they go forth,
that peace may come,
that creation may be healed,
and that those who cry for justice
may be heard. Amen.

# SENDING FORTH

**BENEDICTION** *(Romans 15)*
May the God of love fill you with joy and peace.
May the peace of Christ be with you,
now and forevermore.
And may the Holy Spirit fill your days with hope.
Amen.

Notes

# December 14, 2025

## Third Sunday of Advent

### Amy B. Hunter

## COLOR

Purple

## SCRIPTURE READINGS

Isaiah 35; Luke 1:47-55; James 5:7-10; Matthew 11:2-11

## THEME IDEAS

The Third Sunday of Advent cries out for us to *Rejoice!* While the call to rejoice may seem straight-forward, it is not always easy. The foundation of our Advent joy, indeed of our Advent waiting and preparation, is fierce hope and profound patience. By trusting God's extravagant promises of justice and mercy, we strengthen one another, as we yearn for restoration and everlasting joy. Taking our cue from Nature's slow unfolding of the seasons, we are called to be patient, knowing that we can neither hurry nor fully understand God's work in human history.

# INVITATION AND GATHERING

*CENTERING WORDS (Isaiah 35)*

Wait together for God, trusting the Advent journey. Walk this Holy Way, trusting the One who promises us joy, the One who keeps us from going astray.

*CALL TO WORSHIP (Isaiah 35, Luke 1, James 5, Matthew 11)*

We gather today in great hope,
longing to see the glory of the Lord,
the majesty of our God.
  **The Almighty has done great things for us.**
  **Holy is God's name.**
May our worship strengthen our hands,
make firm our trembling knees,
and unburden our fearful hearts.
  **The Almighty has done great things for us.**
  **Holy is God's name.**
Knowing that God is near, let us be patient
with the times and with one another.
  **The Almighty has done great things for us.**
  **Holy is God's name.**
To all who ask about our hope,
let us tell the good news
of what we have seen and heard.
  **The Almighty has done great things for us.**
  **Holy is God's name.**

*OPENING PRAYER (Isaiah 35, James 5, Matthew 11)*

Joyful and patient God,
    you break into our Advent busyness
      with your extravagant promise
        of glory and joy.

Fire up our imaginations with holy trust
in your goodness.
Inspire us with a patience
that sees beyond our habitual longing
for past glories and understandings.
Move us beyond our too familiar criticisms
of one another and of ourselves.
Open our eyes and help us see your compassion,
already at work in our world:
healing, restoring, strengthening,
and telling the good news that you are near.
Make us signs of your everlasting joy
for your people and for all the world
We pray in the name of Jesus,
whose nearness we proclaim. Amen.

# PROCLAMATION AND RESPONSE

*PRAYER OF YEARNING (Isaiah 35, Luke 1, James 5, Matthew 11)*
Advent God, we yearn to rejoice,
as we tell of Jesus coming into our world.
We long to see your promise
of mercy, justice, and restoration,
fulfilled for all people everywhere.
In our yearning, we discover that our hands are weak,
our knees are feeble,
and our hearts are full of fear.
Stuck in old stories and remembered glories,
we grow critical of one another and of ourselves.
We even wonder whether Jesus is near.
Then our desire to rejoice sputters
in frustration and impatience.

Restore us, yearned-for God.
>for your joy is not our accomplishment,
>>but your gift.
Set us on the Holy Way of Advent,
>forgiven, strengthened, and healed,
>>rejoicing in your glory and majesty. Amen.

## WORDS OF ASSURANCE (Isaiah 35)

Advent People of God, as those ransomed by the Lord,
>walk the Holy Way, where no traveler goes astray.
Come, rejoicing and singing,
>knowing that sorrow and sighing shall flee
>and that God's everlasting joy
>shall surround and hold you.

## PASSING THE PEACE OF CHRIST (Isaiah 35, Luke 1, James 5, Matthew 11)

Beloved people, as those who are called to rejoice while
we await the coming of our Lord, share God's peace and
be at peace with one another.

## INTRODUCTION TO THE WORD (Matthew 11)

We ask that God's Holy Word might prepare our hearts
and minds to know that Jesus is the one we seek in this
season of Advent.

## RESPONSE TO THE WORD (Matthew 11)

In God's word, we hear and see the good news
>of Jesus Christ.

# THANKSGIVING AND COMMUNION

### INVITATION TO THE OFFERING (Isaiah 35, Luke 1, James 5, Matthew 11)

With rejoicing and patience, we not only wait for the coming of God's kingdom, we work to make God's kingdom known. May the gifts we offer today reflect our trust in God, who promises and gives us more than we can even imagine.

### OFFERING PRAYER (Luke 1, James 5)

Generous God who calls us to rejoice,
    you fill the hungry with good things
        and you help your people in need.
Receive the gifts we offer, we pray,
    and make them, and us, joyful and patient signs
        of your coming justice and glory. Amen.

# SENDING FORTH

### BENEDICTION (Isaiah 35, Luke 1, James 5, Matthew 11)

May God, who makes the desert blossom,
    fill you with the joy of God's glory and majesty.
May Jesus, who brings good news to all people,
    fill you with the joy of patience,
        as you await the coming of the Lord.
May the Holy Spirit, who keeps God's promises
    of mercy and justice, fill you with the joy of hope,
        as you walk the Holy Way of Advent. Amen.

# Notes

# December 21, 2025

## Fourth Sunday of Advent

Sara Lambert

## COLOR

Purple

## SCRIPTURE READINGS

Isaiah 7:10-16; Psalm 80:1-7, 17-19; Romans 1:1-7;
Matthew 1:18-25

## THEME IDEAS

There are signs throughout these passages. Although
Ahaz is afraid to hear it, Isaiah tells of a sign of God's
favor—a child will be born to a young woman of his
household. This prophecy becomes hope to early Christians and continues today as a foretelling Christ's birth.
Psalm 80 includes the invocation: "Restore us, O Lord
God of hosts, let your face shine" (v.3). Paul talks about
Christ's descent from David, and proclaims him to be
the Son of God, as proved by his resurrection. Exhorting
others to take the faith to Gentiles as well as to Jews,
Paul says that all people belong to Christ—a sign of the
spread of Christianity. Matthew's story of Jesus' birth
focuses on Joseph and his dream of an angel telling him
to accept Mary as his wife, despite her pregnancy. His

devoted faith in God's word, and his decision to take the foster father role, matches Mary's decision to carry the child. This is another sign that they are made for each other and are prepared to follow God's promise.

# INVITATION AND GATHERING

**CENTERING WORDS** *(Isaiah 7, Romans 1, Psalm 80, Matthew 1)*

Preparing for the arrival of love, center your prayers on Emmanuel—God with us—and the beauty to come. With open hearts and lifted hands, breathe deeply, as you wait for signs of Christ's coming.

**CALL TO WORSHIP** *(Isaiah 7, Psalm 80, Romans 1, Matthew 1)*

The signs are there: God's love comes again,
showering us with the light of Christ!
    **O Lord God of hosts, let your face shine,**
    **that we may be saved.**
With anticipation of the divine, we remain expectant
and marvel at the steadfast faith of Mary and Joseph.
    **O Lord God of hosts, let your face shine,**
    **that we may be saved.**
The time is nearly upon us.
Preparations are almost complete.
Are we ready for change?
    **O Lord God of hosts, let your face shine,**
    **that we may be saved.**
Worship and praise God for these signs
of hope and love!
    **O Lord God of hosts, let your face shine,**
    **that we may be saved.**

**OPENING PRAYER** *(Matthew 1, Isaiah 7, Romans 1, Psalm 80)*

In this season of love, hope and family,
    grant us joy and peace this day.
You offered signs to Joseph and Mary long ago—
    signs that their son would be the Messiah,
        Emmanuel.
May your light shine on us here,
    that we might understand the signs in our lives.
We come with open hearts and minds
    to hear of your love coming into the world.
We come to hear of a young woman with child,
    a foster father with trust in God,
        a match you made in heaven
            to shepherd a tiny boy to his destiny.
Holy God, show us your peace
    as we make ready for your light in the world!

# PROCLAMATION AND RESPONSE

**PRAYER OF YEARNING** *(Psalm 80, Isaiah 7, Matthew 1, Romans 1)*

We lay our burdens before you, O Lord,
    with our lives open and ready to receive
        your light and love.
Lead us toward your Son, Jesus, Emmanuel,
    as we continue to wander with you in faith.
Thank you for the many signs of your love,
    sent in your infinite wisdom.
May we have the faith of Mary and Joseph,
    and may we be your attendants,
        anxious for the coming of your light
            once again. Amen.

**WORDS OF ASSURANCE (Isaiah 7, Psalm 80, Romans 1, Matthew 1)**
The king of love comes for all!
With tears wiped away and replaced with joy,
delight in preparing for the imminent arrival
of the Son of God.
We are all called by God, forgiven, cleansed,
and made free.

**PASSING THE PEACE OF CHRIST (Matthew 1, Romans 1)**
May Christ's peace fill you with joy during this season
of hope. May signs of God's love bring peace and serenity, as you await the birth of light.

**RESPONSE TO THE WORD (Matthew 1, Romans 1, Psalm 80)**
From the prophecy of Isaiah
to the announcement of Christ's birth,
we prepare for Christ's coming—
the coming of light into the world.
With Joseph's example of quiet obedience
and faithful humility,
we endeavor to faithfully follow God's word.
We are part of the family of God,
adopted into the hope of God's faithfulness,
brought into the light of God coming into the world.

# THANKSGIVING AND COMMUNION

**OFFERING PRAYER (Psalm 80, Matthew 1, Romans 1)**
Lord of Heaven, accept these gifts from our hearts,
that they may fulfill the purposes of your people.
As Christ's light shines upon us,
we rejoice in the opportunity to share our abundance
with others.
Bless these offerings to the Christ child
and to our resurrected Lord.

# SENDING FORTH

**BENEDICTION** (*Matthew 1, Psalm 80, Isaiah 7, Romans 1*)
Go in faith and anticipation of the greatest gift of all.
Christ, the Light of the World, will restore us
   to love, hope, and peace.
Emmanuel, God with us, will be with us again.
With faithful obedience encouraging us,
   let us happily await the days ahead.
Go in joy to spread signs of God's good news.

Notes

# December 24, 2025

## Christmas Eve

### Hans Holznagel

## COLOR

White

## SCRIPTURE READINGS

Isaiah 9:2-7; Psalm 96; Titus 2:11-14; Luke 2:1-20

## THEME IDEAS

Fields and seas. Heavens and trees. Flocks and a manger. It seems the joyous birth of Light is not just for all people, but for all the earth. Amid human conflict and a burdened climate, may God's people today bear good news, be zealous for good deeds, and train for new habits in harmony with God's firmly established world. And may the earth rejoice.

## INVITATION AND GATHERING

**CENTERING WORDS** (*Luke 2, Psalm 96*)
Tonight God enters, again, a trembling world. Let all the earth rejoice!

**CALL TO WORSHIP** *(Titus 2, Psalm 96, Luke 2)*
Behold! Our God, earth's maker, appears anew.
**Let all the earth declare God's marvelous works.**
A Word arrives from skies and fields, a message
for a world beset by conflict, fire, flood and storm.
**The heavens are glad! The earth rejoices!**
**The seas roar! The trees sing!**
This is good news, heralding the coming reign of peace
for all creation.
**Sing a new song of God's glory and strength,**
**of lives made new! Let us worship God.**

**OPENING PRAYER** *(Luke 2, Isaiah 9, Titus 2, Psalm 96)*
This bright night is for mystery, O God.
We scarcely understand the ways
you break into this world and into our lives.
Yet we know you do.
The whole earth still needs your peace,
with peoples in conflict and climate in crisis.
May the ancient story of your arrival this night
make us courageous bearers of good news
and doers of good deeds.
For the sake of your beautiful, created world we pray.
Amen.

# PROCLAMATION AND RESPONSE

**PRAYER OF YEARNING** *(Isaiah 9, Psalm 96, Titus 2, Luke 2)*
Burdens press us hard, O God.
We yearn for harmony:
with one another, among races and nations,
and with the earth you have created.

Where idols distract us
from you and your marvelous works,
help us make a change.
Send us good news of great joy, we pray. Amen.

*WORDS OF ASSURANCE (Isaiah 9, Luke 2, Titus 2)*
Our ancestors saw a great light.
So, too, do grace and peace descend upon us now.
They are already here.
They are gifts of God, the Wonderful Counselor,
the lifter of burdens and oppressions.
Grace has appeared, bringing salvation. Amen.

*PASSING THE PEACE OF CHRIST (Isaiah 9, Luke 2)*
In the name of the Prince of Peace—Jesus, born in a manger this night—let us greet one another with signs of peace. The peace of Christ be with you.

*RESPONSE TO THE WORD (Luke 2, Titus 2, Psalm 96)*
May God's Word redeem us, increasing our zeal
for the renewal of all the earth.

# THANKSGIVING AND COMMUNION

*INVITATION TO THE OFFERING (Luke 2, Psalm 96)*
As it once appeared in ancient fields, the mystery of God's glory shines around us again this Christmas Eve. Like shepherds of old, let us respond with good news. With the psalmist, let us bring offerings of our lives and resources. And may the heavens be glad and the earth rejoice.

**OFFERING PRAYER *(Titus 2, Psalm 96)***
Creator God, may these gifts—
offered for good work throughout the world—
ascribe glory and strength to you. Amen.

# SENDING FORTH

**BENEDICTION *(Luke 2, Titus 2)***
People of God, you have heard the good news
of great joy.
It is real. It is for all the earth.
Go forth, bearing this news.
And may all who hear it and see it,
reveal this good news in their lives,
and be amazed.

Notes

# December 28, 2025

## First Sunday after Christmas

### Mary Scifres
*Copyright © Mary Scifres*

## COLOR

White

## SCRIPTURE READINGS

Isaiah 63:7-9; Psalm 148; Hebrews 2:10-18;
Matthew 2:13-23

## THEME IDEAS

The focus on suffering, just a few days into the Christmas
season, seems antithetical to our traditions of worship
and celebration in this season. Yet, suffering is the back-
drop of the Christmas story. Even our bright, Christmas
Eve celebrations tell only part of the story. Even Luke's
birth story of angels and heavenly songs is a story of
lowly shepherds visiting an unwed teenage mother giving birth in a cave. In Matthew's story, the worship of
foreign kings is accompanied by an escape from King
Herod, who sought to kill anyone who threatened his
power. Suffering is a part of our story too. Even as we
celebrate Christ's birth, we remember his humble beginnings, the diverse followers he invites onto the journey,

and the suffering that came at the hands of those whose power was threatened by the leader who led with love and servanthood.

# INVITATION AND GATHERING

**CENTERING WORDS (Isaiah 63, Hebrews 2, Matthew 2)**
How can we sing Christ's praise in an imperfect world? By remembering that we are lifted, carried, and redeemed by God's perfect love.

**CALL TO WORSHIP (Psalm 148)**
Praise the God of mercy and love.
**Praise God with angels in the highest heavens.**
Praise Christ, who came as a child.
**Praise Christ with all God's children,**
**young and old alike.**
Praise the Holy Spirit, who calls us here.
**Praise the Spirit from the depths of our souls.**

**OPENING PRAYER (Isaiah 63, Hebrews 2, Matthew 2, Christmas)**
Loving God, we come into your presence
with joy in this holiday season.
But we also come with sorrow
for a world struggling in pain.
Bring hope to our weary world.
Bring love to our hearts.
Bring joy to our lives.
And help us bring hope, love, and joy,
as we follow your Son, Christ Jesus. Amen.

# PROCLAMATION AND RESPONSE

*PRAYER OF YEARNING (Isaiah 63, Hebrews 2, Matthew 2)*

> Merciful God, we yearn to be merciful and gracious,
> > as you have been merciful and gracious to us.
> Grant us the mercy to redeem our lives,
> > and give us the strength to live
> > > as those who are redeemed.
> Help us resist the forces of evil and cruelty
> > that kill our hope and destroy our souls.
> Fill us with your light and love,
> > that we may overflow with mercy, compassion,
> > > help, and hope for our world.
> In your holy name, we pray. Amen.

*WORDS OF ASSURANCE (Isaiah 63)*

> In love and mercy, God redeems us.
> In grace and joy, God lifts us.
> In strength and security,
> > God carries us all the days of our lives.

*RESPONSE TO THE WORD or BENEDICTION (Christmas, Hebrews 2)*

> May the work of Christmas begin with us.
> > **May the work of discipleship guide our lives.**
> May the gifts of mercy and grace flow through us.
> > **May praise and joy strengthen our journey.**
> May Christ light the way.

# THANKSGIVING AND COMMUNION

**INVITATION TO THE OFFERING** *(Matthew 2, Christmas)*
> Just as visitors from the East brought gifts to the Christ child, we too are invited to bring gifts to Christ's church in service of God's work in the world. Any gift of love is a gift of gold.

**OFFERING PRAYER** *(Christmas)*
> Generous God, thank you for the gift of Christ Jesus
> in our lives and in our world.
> Thank you for the gifts we return to you now.
> Bless these gifts,
> that they may support Christ's loving presence
> in our ministry,
> in our community,
> and in our world. Amen.

# SENDING FORTH

**BENEDICTION** *(Isaiah 63, Hebrews 2)*
> In love and mercy, God sends us forth.
> **In love and mercy, we go to serve.**
> Let Christ lead the way.

# Notes

# Contributors

**B. J. Beu** is a UCC pastor, spiritual director, and coach who has served churches in the United Church of Christ and United Methodist Church for over twenty-five years. B. J. lives in Laguna Beach with his wife, Mary.

**Michael Beu** is a professional film editor, serving as the tech director for Shepherd of the Hills United Methodist Church and worship editor for various other churches in California. www.elementproductions.net.

**Mary Petrina Boyd** is pastor of Marysville United Methodist Church, northeast of Seattle. She spends alternating summers working as an archaeologist in Jordan.

**Anna Crews Camphouse** is an ordained Elder in the United Methodist Church serving churches in Northwest Connecticut. She loves inter-cultural, inter-spiritual, and globally-conscious ministry, embodying a special affinity for listening practices and meaning-making conversations.

**James Dollins** is Senior Pastor of San Marcos United Methodist Church in Southern California, where he lives with his wife, Serena, and sons, Forrest and Silas. He is a lover of music, intercultural ministries, and God's creation.

**Karin Ellis** is a United Methodist pastor who lives with her husband and children in La Cañada, California. She enjoys writing liturgy for worship and children's stories.

**Rebecca J. Kruger Gaudino**, a United Church of Christ minister in Portland, Oregon, teaches biblical studies and theology at the University of Portland and also writes for the church.

**Hans Holznagel** has worked as a newspaper reporter, helped run a theater, served on the staff of a residence for low-income adults, and worked for the national ministries of the United Church of Christ in communications, mission education, administration, and fundraising. Recently retired, he and his wife, Kathy Harlow, live on Cleveland's Near West Side, where they belong to Archwood UCC.

**Amy B. Hunter** is a religious educator and spiritual director in Lowell, Massachusetts. She is an Episcopal layperson who loves liturgy and the occasional opportunity to preach.

**Sara Dunning Lambert** enjoys retired life with friends and family, especially her grandkids. She is an occasional worship leader at Bear Creek UMC in Woodinville, Washington.

**Kirsten Linford** serves as senior minister of Westwood Hills Congregational (UCC) church and preschool in Los Angeles. She shares her life with her young daughter, Riley, and their golden retriever, Seamus. Ecumenism is in her blood. Pastoring and parenting with a UCC head and a Disciples of Christ heart, she is delighted to be writing for a United Methodist publishing house.

**Silvia Purdie** is a counsellor and a minister of the Presbyterian Church of Aotearoa New Zealand. She also offers training and leadership resources for climate change and sustainability. Access her extensive collection of resources and her book on Women in Creation Care at www.conversations.net.nz.

**Mary J. Scifres** is a United Methodist pastor serving as a leadership coach, consultant, and author. Learn more at www.maryscifres.com.

**Rev. Dr. Leigh Ann Shaw** is an ordained elder in The United Methodist Church, who lives in Carlsbad, California. She loves writing and exploring and advocating for those without a voice.

**Kristiane Smith** is a United Methodist pastor serving in Southern California. Her passions include creative writing, music, hanging out with her husband and three teens, and helping others examine and make sense of their faith journey.

**Leigh Anne Taylor** walks alongside her husband, Hugh, and their five children and four grandchildren as a blessed "LaLa" among the clergy and churches of the Mountain View District in south central Virginia as Director of Connecting Ministries. She loves learning about the Enneagram of the Soul and spiritual practices.

**Michelle L. Torigian** is a pastor at St. Paul United Church of Christ in Belleville, Illinois, and blogs at michelletorigian.com. Her passions in the arts include painting and woodburning, as well as writing prayers and liturgies.

# Scripture Index

## Old Testament

# New Testament

SCRIPTURE INDEX

12:1-11 ........................17
12:12-31a ...................22
13:1-13 ........................27
15:1-11 ........................34
15:12-20 .....................39
15:19-26 .....................103
15:35-38, 42-50 ...........44

**2 Corinthians**
3:12–4:2 ......................49
5:20b–6:10 ..................56
5:16-21 ........................75

**Galatians**
3:23-29 ........................148
5:1, 13-25 ...................152
6:(1-6) 7-16 ................157

**Ephesians**
1:11-23 ........................244
1:15-23 ........................133
3:1-12 ..........................5

**Philippians**
2:5-11 ..........................85
3:4b-14 .......................80
3:17–4:1 ......................66
4:4-9 ...........................265

**Colossians**
1:1-14 ..........................163
1:11-20 ........................260
1:15-28 ........................168
2:6-15, (16-19) ............173
3:1-11 ..........................178

**2 Thessalonians**
2:1-5, 13-17 ................249
3:6-13 ..........................254

**1 Timothy**
1:12-17 ........................209
2:1-7 ...........................215
6:6-19 ..........................219

**2 Timothy**
1:1-14 ..........................224
2:8-15 ..........................229
3:14–4:5 ......................234
4:6-8, 16-18 ................239

**Titus**
2:11-14 ........................295

**Philemon**
1-21 ............................203

**Hebrews**
2:10-18 ........................300
10:16-25 ......................98
11:1-3, 8-16 ................183
11:29–12:2 ..................188
12:18-29 ......................193
13:1-8, 15-16 ..............198

**James**
5:7-10 ..........................284

**Revelation**
1:4-8 ...........................109
5:11-14 ........................113
7:9-17 ..........................118
21:1-6 ..........................1
21:1-10, 22–22:5 ..........123, 128
22:12-14, 16-17, 20-21 ........133